D0861236

EVALUATING
CHILDREN
SUSPECTED
OF HAVING
BEEN
SEXUALLY
ABUSED

THE APSAC STUDY GUIDES 2

FLORIDA STATE
UNIVERSITY LIBRARIES

APR 22 1996

TALLAHASSEE, FLORIDA

The APSAC Study Guides

Jon R. Conte, Series Editor

The APSAC Study Guides are intended to provide an outline of critical knowledge in selected aspects of child maltreatment and to direct the reader to important research and other knowledge. Prepared by leading experts in each area, the study guides offer these experts' summaries of important knowledge areas, some critical analysis of the knowledge and issues in each area, and the identification of critical questions raised by the knowledge in the particular area of child maltreatment.

In this series:

Founded in 1987, the American Professional Society on the Abuse of Children (APSAC) is the nation's only interdisciplinary professional society for those working in the field of child abuse and neglect. APSAC's mission is to improve society's response to the abuse and neglect of its children by promoting effective interdisciplinary approaches to the identification, intervention, treatment, and prevention of child maltreatment.

American Professional Society on the Abuse of Children
407 S. Dearborn, Suite 1300
Chicago, IL 60605
Phone: 312-554-0166
Fax: 312-554-0919

KATHLEEN
COULBORN
FALLER

EVALUATING

CHILDREN

SUSPECTED

OF HAVING

BEEN

SEXUALLY

ABUSED

THE APSAC STUDY GUIDES 2

APSAC

**Published in cooperation with the
American Professional Society on the
Abuse of Children (APSAC)**

SAGE Publications
International Educational and Professional Publisher
Thousand Oaks   London   New Delhi

Copyright © 1996 by Sage Publications, Inc.

All rights reserved. No part of this book may be reproduced or utilized in any form or by any means, electronic or mechanical, including photocopying, recording, or by any information storage and retrieval system, without permission in writing from the publisher.

For information address:

SAGE Publications, Inc.
2455 Teller Road
Thousand Oaks, California 91320
E-mail: order@sagepub.com

SAGE Publications Ltd.
6 Bonhill Street
London EC2A 4PU
United Kingdom

SAGE Publications India Pvt. Ltd.
M-32 Market
Greater Kailash I
New Delhi 110 048 India

HV
8079
C48
F35
1996

Printed in the United States of America

Library of Congress Cataloging-in-Publication Data

Faller, Kathleen Coulborn.
    Evaluating children suspected of having been sexually abused/
Kathleen Coulborn Faller.
        p. cm.—(APSAC study guides; no. 2)
    ISBN 0-7618-0072-1 (pbk.)
    1. Child sexual abuse—investigation. 2. Interviewing in child
abuse. I. Title. II. Series.
HV8079.C48F35 1996
363.2'59536—dc20   95-32507

96 97 98 99 10 9 8 7 6 5 4 3 2 1

This book is printed on acid-free paper.

Sage Production Editor: Diana E. Axelsen
Sage Typesetter: Danielle Dillahunt
Cover Illustrator: Dawn Anderson

Contents

This Study Guide and the accompanying knowledge test are intended to assist the reader in his or her own professional continuing education. It is the responsibility of the reader to fully and accurately review the entire professional literature that this Study Guide addresses and to base professional actions on the reader's education, training, experience, and supervision. Furthermore, it is the responsibility of the reader of this Study Guide to view this Study Guide and the accompanying knowledge test as only one aspect of continuing professional education. The Study Guide and knowledge test do not certify, credential, license, or make any statement about the reader's skills, knowledge, expertise, or ability to practice in this area. The reader should never so represent to others.

The reader agrees to indemnify and hold harmless the author, editor, The American Professional Society on the Abuse of Children, and Sage Publications against any claim, damage, or loss resulting from or arising out of the reader's use of this Study Guide and the accompanying materials.

Series Editor's Introduction

The APSAC Study Guides were born out of the ongoing commitment of the American Professional Society on the Abuse of Children (APSAC) to provide the latest information, current knowledge, and best ideas about practice to its members and other professionals who work in child maltreatment.

The guides are intended to provide an outline of critical knowledge in selected aspects of child maltreatment and to direct the reader to important research and other knowledge. Prepared by leading experts in each area, the study guides offer these experts' summaries of important knowledge areas, some critical analysis of the knowledge and issues in each area, and the identification of critical questions raised by the knowledge in the particular area of child maltreatment.

It is important to bear in mind what the study guides are not. They are not intended to be a full summary of critical knowledge, research knowledge, or critical analyses of professional research and knowledge. They are not intended to remove the need of the professional to keep current in research and other professional literatures. Neither the guides nor the knowledge tests available from PsychoEducational Resources are intended to be a process for the certification of professionals, knowledge, or specific aspects of practice.

The guides can serve as road maps to important papers, chapters, and articles that readers can obtain in order to pursue topics and explore perspectives. The reader is encouraged to use the study guide as one source for critical comments and points of view about this literature and to see how the reader's own ideas, analysis, or opinions agree or disagree with those of the study guide author.

Knowledge testing is made possible through collaboration with PsychoEducational Resources (PER). The knowledge test, client vignette questions, and related materials are located in a perforated section at the end of the book. Tear out this section, complete the test questions, sign the form verifying your completion of this home study program, complete the program evaluation/participant satisfaction form, and mail these materials to:

PsychoEducational Resources
P. O. Box 2196
Keystone Heights, FL 32656

If you have questions regarding the testing or the awarding of CE credits, call PER at (904) 473-7300.

PER is approved by the American Psychological Association to offer continuing education for psychologists and by the Florida Board of Licensed Clinical Social Work, Marriage and Family Therapy, and Mental Health Counseling (CM #406, '97). PER is also approved by the Connecticut chapter of NASW, and it conforms to the standards of the following states for awarding CE credits to social workers: Alabama, Arkansas, Georgia, Idaho, Kansas, Nebraska, New Hampshire, New Mexico, Oregon, Texas, and West Virginia. These CE sponsorships are honored by many state boards of social work, marriage and family therapy, and professional counseling. Other state approvals are pending. Some restrictions may apply. Check with your state board or call PER at the number above. PER maintains responsibility for these programs and adheres to all sponsorship guidelines for providing CE credits.

Be aware that the knowledge test includes some questions from the key literature to which you are guided in the manual. Six CE credits are awarded with an 80% pass on the tests. Quizzes may be retaken without penalty or additional charge if the pass rate is not met initially. The cost of testing and awarding of CE credit and certificate is included in the price of the book.

APSAC is the nation's only interdisciplinary society for professionals working in the field of child abuse and neglect. One of APSAC's primary aims is to ensure that everyone affected by child maltreatment receives the best possible professional response. To that end, APSAC produces a wide range of professional publications, including the quarterly journal, *Child Maltreatment*; the quarterly newsletter, *The APSAC Advisor*; guidelines for interdisciplinary professional practice; and *The APSAC Handbook on Child Maltreatment*. **The APSAC Study Guides** series is yet another important avenue through which APSAC seeks to implement its commitment to ongoing professional education.

JON R. CONTE
University of Washington

Acknowledgments

This study guide is one of several that has been fostered and sponsored by the American Professional Society on the Abuse of Children (APSAC). This endeavor owes a great deal to the initiative, conceptualization, and editorship of Jon Conte, PhD, the first president of APSAC and a pioneer in the sexual abuse field. Moreover, this book would not have seen publication without the support of Terry Hendrix of Sage Publications and the interest of Sage in the advancement of knowledge related to family violence.

Although the author conducted the initial review of the literature and draft of the manuscript, the quality of the work has been immeasurably enhanced by peer review of professionals who are also members of APSAC and experts in the child interview process (Lucy Berliner, MSW; Mark Everson, PhD; and Charles Wilson, MSW). Thus, this study guide reflects not only the author's synthesis and interpretation of the current state of the field regarding interviewing children who may have been sexually abused but the input of other experts in the field. Their wisdom and observations in some instances can be referenced by publications, but in others cannot. In the latter situations, I have cited them by name and indicated the source as "personal communication."

In addition, members of the board of directors of APSAC had an opportunity to review the completed manuscript and decide whether it reflected the APSAC position regarding child interviews in suspected sexual abuse. Consequently, this document reflects much more than the author's observations and interpretation of the state of knowledge about children suspected of being sexually abused. For this, I am indebted.

Introduction

A good deal of controversy has arisen during the past 12 years about how to tell whether a child has been sexually abused, once abuse is suspected. This issue has been addressed in the literature, which consists of articles based on research findings, clinical experience, and authors' opinions. Assessment of sexual abuse also has been the subject of conference presentations, which may be data based or derived from clinical experience. Finally, the problem of deciding if sexual abuse happened is reflected in efforts to develop good practice, which often are not published. Because this study guide is essentially a critical review of the literature, its emphasis will be on what has been written. However, at various junctures, unpublished work and clinical practice, with appropriate information so the reader can obtain written documents and further information, will be cited because of their relevance to the topic discussed.

Because, at this time, the preponderance of evaluators look on data related to the child as the most important in substantiating or not substantiating suspected sexual abuse, the focus of the study guide will be on the alleged victim and how to gather and assess information from and about the child. Therefore, for example, the study guide will not address the issue of offender assessment or characteristics, nor will it describe environmental or family factors that might increase risk of sexual abuse. Moreover, the study guide will limit itself to psychosocial findings and victim statements and behavior. It will not consider medical and other physical evidence. However, models for evaluation that go beyond the child assessment process will be described and their utility discussed.

The intended audience is the broad spectrum of service providers who are involved in child interviewing and assessment, which can include health care professionals, child protection workers, law enforcement personnel, and prosecutors, but the major focus of the study guide will be on information particularly relevant to mental health professionals. Some of the methods described, for example, psychological tests, would not be used by prosecutors, child protection workers, or law enforcement personnel.

The study guide will be divided by chapter into knowledge areas. For most knowledge areas, basic references will be listed and their contents briefly described. A complete reference section can be found at the end of each chapter. For the reader to master the material discussed, all references, basic and not basic, should be reviewed.

Objectives

A. To acquaint the reader with the substantive areas that are fundamental to assessing an allegation of child sexual abuse. Knowledge areas to be covered include the following:

1. Models for evaluating abuse
2. Interviewer objectivity
3. Number of child interviews
4. Documentation
5. Standardized tests
6. Questioning techniques
7. Media for interviewing children
   a. Anatomical dolls
   b. Anatomical drawings
   c. Picture drawing
8. Evaluations of very young children
9. Children as witnesses
10. False allegations of sexual abuse
11. Criteria for deciding whether an allegation is true
12. Formulating conclusions

B. To better enable the reader to evaluate the research studies and the conceptual, clinical, and conclusory writings related to assessing suspected child sexual abuse.

C. To inform the reader about how to conduct an adequate evaluation of suspected sexual abuse.

D. To prepare the reader to defend her or his evaluation procedures in the court and other arenas.

Models for Evaluating
Child Sexual Abuse

Basic References

American Professional Society on the Abuse of Children (APSAC). (1990). *Guidelines for psychosocial evaluation of suspected sexual abuse in young children.* (Available from APSAC, 407 S. Dearborn Ave., Suite 1300, Chicago, IL 60605.)

These guidelines evolved by consensus among APSAC experts, members who conduct evaluations of children alleged to have been sexually abused, and other interested parties. They were reviewed and amended several times before their publication and continue to be subject to periodic review. The APSAC guidelines contain sections on the qualifications of the evaluator, the components of an evaluation, interviewing procedures, interview techniques, and conclusions and the written report. They are applicable to both intrafamilial and extrafamilial sexual abuse.

American Academy of Child and Adolescent Psychiatry (AACAP). (1990, December). *Guidelines for the evaluation of child and adolescent sexual abuse.* (Available from AACAP, 3615 Wisconsin Ave. N.W., Washington, DC 20016.)

The AACAP guidelines were developed by a subcommittee of the AACAP Committee on Rights and Legal Matters, composed of nine child psychiatrists with the assistance of four outside consultants who are not child psychiatrists. They are more applicable to allegations of sexual abuse in divorce cases and are less helpful in assessing the full spectrum of sexual abuse cases. They do not seem to be intended for use in cases of extrafamilial sexual abuse. These guidelines express a preference that sexual abuse evaluations be conducted by psychiatrists or psychologists or skilled clinicians under their supervision. Like the APSAC guidelines, these are subject to periodic review and are currently being revised.

They contain the following sections: choice of clinician to evaluate the child, number of interviews, location of the interviews, obtaining a history, interviewing both parents in intrafamilial abuse, use of *guardian ad litem*, considering false allegations, modifications in the clinical evaluation, assessing the child's credibility, anatomically correct dolls, use of children's drawings, videotaping, psychological testing, reporting, medical evaluation, and formulating recommendations.

Conte, J., Sorenson, E., Fogarty, L., & Dalla Rosa, J. (1991). Evaluating children's reports of sexual abuse: Results from a survey of professionals. *American Journal of Orthopsychiatry, 61,* 428-437.

Conte and colleagues surveyed 212 experts in child sexual abuse from 40 states, asking specifically about how they assess children suspected of having been sexually abused, what criteria they use in determining the validity of an allegation, the relative importance of these criteria, and what they consider characteristic of false allegations. Like the APSAC guidelines, the results of this study represent a consensus among experts.

Hibbard, R. A., & Hartmann, G. A. (1993). Components of child and parent interviews in cases of alleged sexual abuse. *Child Abuse & Neglect, 17,* 495-500.

This is an empirical study of the interview practices of 214 medical personnel, social workers, legal personnel, and psychologists, asking about types of information they seek during parent and child interviews regarding possible sexual abuse. The researchers were queried about the following: details of the abuse, family relations, school, child development, child's names for body parts, child's knowledge about body part functions, child-rearing practices, medical history, behavior problems, psychological symptoms, physical complaints, parental teaching about sex, and access to sexually explicit material. Some topics were covered by many respondents, for example, details of the abuse, family relations, and various child abuse symptoms. However, as might be expected, there were significant differences among professionals regarding the likelihood of discussion of other topics.

Morgan, M., with Edwards, V. (1995). *How to interview sexual abuse victims: Including the use of anatomical dolls.* Thousand Oaks, CA: Sage.

This is a basic and very practical text by the original developers of anatomical dolls on child interviewing in cases of possible sexual abuse. Although this book is practice rather than research based, it provides a review of anatomical doll research in an appendix and reflects experience with anatomical dolls nationally.

Everson, M. (1992, January). *Models of sexual abuse evaluations.* Presentation given at the conference on the Health Science Response to Child Maltreatment, San Diego, CA. (Summary available from Mark Everson, Program on Childhood Abuse and Trauma, Department of Psychiatry, CB 7160, University of North Carolina, Chapel Hill, NC 27599-7160.)

Everson is responsible for the conceptualization of current practice into three models. He described these models and their underlying assumptions regarding substantiation of child sexual abuse at the above-cited presentation.

STUDY QUESTION

1. What are the six basic references cited by the author?

Review and Critique

During the past 12 years, different models have evolved for evaluating allegations of sexual abuse, and no doubt there will be continued evolution of such models. Current practice is conceptualized here into three different models. Their special characteristics, origins, and assumptions will be discussed.

Child Interview Model

The essential component of this model is the interview or interviews with the suspected victim. Because most children do not come to an evaluation on their own, the accompanying adult is usually also interviewed to gather information about the child and the allegation. When conducted in medical settings, an additional component of the model is a medical evaluation. The model derives primarily from the mandate of child protective services. Protective services is typically faced with a complaint of possible sexual abuse, which it must investigate. By the process of trial and error and the application of common sense, it became apparent that the best source of data to substantiate or deny the allegation is the child. The research of Conte et al. (1991) and Hibbard and Hartmann (1993), as well as the manual of Morgan (1995), reflect this perspective.

Mental health professionals became the providers of these kinds of evaluations because of mandated investigators' lack of training, time, and credentials that could withstand the scrutiny of the court. However, in many communities, child protection workers and law enforcement personnel conduct investigative interviews that are as sophisticated as those provided by mental health professionals (Morgan, 1995).

Although psychological testing of the child is sometimes a component of the child interview model, it is considered an adjunct to information elicited more directly, for example, by interviewing and using anatomical dolls, picture drawing, or anatomical drawings (APSAC, 1990).

Some programs employing this model forbid the alleged offender from coming to the facility because it is felt that his or her presence will prevent the child from believing the facility is a safe place to disclose, if there is anything to disclose (Center for Child Protection, 1992). Moreover, most adherents of this model assume that any interview of the victim with the alleged offender will be both counterproductive to disclosure and, if it occurs after the child interview, perceived by the child as another betrayal or violation of trust, this time by the evaluator (Faller, Froning, & Lipovsky, 1991).

This model is applicable to both intrafamilial and extrafamilial sexual abuse cases.

Some of the assumptions inherent in this model are that children are usually reliable when they give accounts of their sexual abuse and that they rarely make false allegations. In contrast, offenders and nonoffending parents, in intrafamilial abuse cases, often have vested interests in concealing the sexual abuse (Faller, 1988). In addition, this model assumes that there is no single offender profile, and that many offenders cannot be easily differentiated from nonoffending individuals.

To date, this appears to be the most widely used and accepted model for determining the validity of an allegation of sexual abuse (see Conte et al., 1991; Hibbard & Hartmann, 1993).

Parent-Child Interaction Model

In the 1970s and 1980s, some clinicians trying to understand the causes of child maltreatment came to the conclusion that it represented an absence of bonding between parent and child, and that this was manifest in the way parents interacted with their children. This theory was especially applied to children with failure to thrive and battered-child syndrome. For example, clinicians reported that parents whose children failed to thrive did not engage in eye contact; did not hold the child in the *en face* position; and failed to vocalize, for instance, by making cooing noises to the child. Battered children were often described as hypervigilant and avoidant of parental contact. Their parents were noted to speak in a negative tone of voice to their children and to handle them roughly (Haynes-Seman & Hart, 1988).

When clinicians applied this model to sexual abuse, they assumed victims and offenders would engage in sexualized interaction while being observed and/or the child would avoid contact with the sexually abusive parent. In addition, Wehrspann, Steinhauer, and Klajner-Diamond (1987) have suggested that observing how the child behaves both with and without the accused parent will be instructive in differentiating true from false allegations. Authors disagree about the significance and meaning of various reactions of the suspected victim to face-to-face contact with the suspected offender. As previously noted, Faller and colleagues (1991) have disputed the utility and the ethics of an assessment model that includes such a session. Nevertheless, it is assumed by those using this model that parent-child interactions will be readily interpretable by skilled mental health professionals (Haynes-Seman & Baumgarten, 1994; Haynes-Seman & Hart, 1988; Haynes-Seman & Krugman, 1989).

Generally, clinicians employing the parent-child interaction model rely on other techniques in addition to the parent-child interview. An evaluation of this sort would usually include review of background material, an interview with each parent, and interview with the child, as well as an observation of the interaction between the child and each parent. An unusual version of this model is that advocated by Haynes-Seman, which actually has the child present during the assessment of each parent, in addition to a parent-child session with the interviewer absent (Haynes-Seman & Hart, 1988). Some clinicians allow the accused parent to confront the child regarding the allegations of abuse, or the clinician asks the child about the allegation in the presence of the accused parent. This model assumes there is an accusing and an accused parent and has been used primarily when allegations of abuse are made in the context of a divorce.

Although some research has been conducted to ascertain the ability of clinicians to differentiate abusive from nonabusive relationships, it is not entirely supportive of this approach. Starr (1987), in a study involving 23 mental health professionals, with an average of 15 years of experience, and 45 psychology undergraduates, found that both groups could only differentiate at chance levels (50% of the time) between abusive and nonabusive parent-child dyads involved in free-play situations. A comparable study of 52 child welfare workers conducted by Deitrich-MacLean and Walden (1988) found them somewhat more skilled, being able to correctly classify mother-child dyads involved in a task 76% of the time. However, only one case in these two studies involved sexual abuse.

In contrast, Madonna, Van Scoyk, and Jones (1991), in a study of 30 incest families and 30 families with a child referred to a psychiatric clinic, were able to differentiate incest from nonincest families in ratings on the Beavers-Timberlawn Family Evaluation Scale, an instrument that taps family competency along 13 dimensions. The incest families were significantly more dysfunctional overall and rated more pathological on 12 of the 13 dimensions. None of the dimensions relates directly to sexually abusive behavior, and at this point the Beavers-Timberlawn is not structured in such a way as to guide the decision making of mental health staff, child protective services, or law enforcement.

Assumptions of the parent-child interaction model are that actions speak louder that words; that is, more can be learned about sexual abuse allegations from observing the parent-child interaction than from the children's statements. Their statements about sexual abuse cannot be relied on, because children can be coached or may lie about sexual abuse, and many allegations are false (Everson, 1992). A further assumption is that children will not be unduly traumatized by having to deal with confronting an accused parent.

This model is not widely espoused by clinicians evaluating sexual abuse allegations. For example, Conte and colleagues (1991) found that 96% of the experts responding to their study did not interview the child in the presence of the offender. However, a model that includes observation of the parent-child interaction is the model of choice in making decisions about custody and visitation in divorce where there are no allegations of maltreatment.

Comprehensive Evaluation Model

To a considerable extent, the comprehensive evaluation model has evolved because of criticisms, especially in court, of simpler models. However, it also has its origins in a tradition of comprehensive family evaluations used in the mental health and child welfare fields.

Comprehensive evaluations are often conducted by multidisciplinary teams. The teams consist of physicians, social workers, psychologists, and sometimes psychiatrists and lawyers. Some team members may be experts in child interviewing and child development and others in adult assessment and sex offenders. Medical exams of alleged victims, psychological testing (Risin & McNamara, 1989), and interviews are all generally employed. The team reads and integrates background information, for example, the family's protective services history or past allegations and investigations of abuse by other agencies. Collaboration is sought with mandated agencies, that is, protective services, law enforcement, and the courts, and community professionals who have been involved with the family are consulted. Persons conducting these sorts of evaluations expect to provide expert testimony in court.

This model assumes that the child interview is only one of a variety of types of information that need to be considered. However, the child interview may still be regarded as the most important part of the assessment. Such evaluations generally involve both interviews and psychological testing of family members as needed. In addition to those directly involved in the allegations of sexual abuse, siblings not alleged to have been victimized and others, for example, grandparents and foster parents, may be interviewed. In cases where it is deemed essential to answering the questions posed, parent-child and family interactions may be undertaken. However, such sessions would not be central to decision making.

It is evident from the description that this model is suited to allegations of intrafamilial sexual abuse and is not necessary for most allegations of extrafamilial sexual abuse. Its scope makes it particularly indicated for complex cases, where there may be allegations of multiple offenders and/or victims, where the family dysfunction includes a variety of problems, and where there may have been prior evaluations, which were inconclusive or whose conclusions are disputed. Moreover, the model is generally used to provide more information than the answer to the question, "has the child been sexually abused?" Typically, it can address the issues of the type of treatment needed for the offending and nonoffending parent and their prognoses, treatment and placement needs of the victim, the advisability of ultimate family reunification, and the effect and possible success of criminal prosecution.

The drawbacks to this model are the time it takes, its cost, and its intrusiveness into family life. Nevertheless, the research of Hibbard and Hartmann (1993) leads them to support a multidisciplinary approach so that all relevant components of evaluation of a sexual abuse allegation are explored. Moreover, a study by Kaufman, Jones, Steiglitz, and Mannarino (1994) of 56 children, which examined information from child protection workers, parents, medical records, and observations of parent-child interactions, supports the importance of using multiple sources of data. The participants in this study were children referred to an intervention/research project because they had been maltreated. Of the 13 children in this study who were substantiated as sexually abused, 5 had not been so identified before referral to the research.

STUDY QUESTIONS

2. Current practice is conceptualized into what three models?

   a. Briefly describe the essential components and assumptions of each model.

   b. To date, which model appears to be the most widely used and accepted model for evaluating allegations of sexual abuse?

   c. How has the parent-child interaction model been criticized? When does it seem to be the model of choice?

   d. Which model seems indicated for the more complex cases, especially involving allegations of intrafamilial sexual abuse?

References

American Academy of Child and Adolescent Psychiatry (AACAP). (1990, December). *Guidelines for the evaluation of child and adolescent sexual abuse.* (Available from AACAP, 3615 Wisconsin Ave. N.W., Washington, DC 20016)

American Professional Society on the Abuse of Children (APSAC). (1990). *Guidelines for psychosocial evaluation of suspected sexual abuse in young children.* (Available from APSAC, 407 S. Dearborn, Suite 1300, Chicago, IL 60605)

Center for Child Protection. (1992). *Sexual abuse evidentiary protocol.* (Available from the Center for Child Protection, Children's Hospital and Health Center, San Diego, CA 92123)

Conte, J., Sorenson, E., Fogarty, L., & Dalla Rosa, J. (1991). Evaluating children's reports of sexual abuse: Results from a survey of professionals. *American Journal of Orthopsychiatry, 61,* 428-437.

Deitrich-MacLean, G., & Walden, T. (1988). Distinguishing teaching interactions of physically abusive from nonabusive parent-child dyads. *Child Abuse and Neglect, 12,* 469-480.

Everson, M. (1992, January). *Models of sexual abuse evaluations.* Presentation given at the conference on the Health Science Response to Child Maltreatment, San Diego, CA. (Summary available from Mark Everson, Program on Childhood Abuse and Trauma, Department of Psychiatry, CB 7160, University of North Carolina, Chapel Hill, NC 27599-7160)

Faller, K. C. (1988). *Child sexual abuse: An interdisciplinary manual for diagnosis, case management, and treatment.* New York: Columbia University Press.

Faller, K., Froning, M., & Lipovsky, J. (1991). The parent-child interview: Use in evaluating child allegations of sexual abuse by a parent. *American Journal of Orthopsychiatry, 61,* 552-557.

Haynes-Seman, C., & Baumgarten, D. (1994). *Children speak for themselves.* New York: Brunner/Mazel.

Haynes-Seman, C., & Hart, J. S. (1988). Interactional assessment: Evaluation of parent-child relationships in abuse and neglect. In D. Bross, R. Krugman, M. Lenherr, D. A. Rosenberg, & B. Schmitt (Eds.), *The new child protection team handbook* (pp. 181-198). New York: Garland.

Haynes-Seman, C., & Krugman, R. (1989). Sexualized attention: Normal interaction or precursor to sexual abuse? *American Journal of Orthopsychiatry, 59,* 238-245.

Hibbard, R. A., & Hartmann, G. A. (1993). Components of child and parent interviews in cases of alleged sexual abuse. *Child Abuse and Neglect, 17,* 495-500.

Kaufman, J., Jones, B., Steiglitz, V., & Mannarino, A. (1994). The use of multiple informants to assess children's maltreatment experiences. *Journal of Family Violence, 9,* 227-248.

Madonna, P., Van Scoyk, S., & Jones, D. P. H. (1991). Family interactions within incest and nonincest families. *American Journal of Psychiatry, 128*(1), 46-49.

Morgan, M., with Edwards, V. (1995). *How to interview sexual abuse victims: Including the use of anatomical dolls.* Thousand Oaks, CA: Sage.

Risin, L., & McNamara, R. (1989). Validation of child sexual abuse: The psychologist's role. *Journal of Clinical Psychology, 45,* 175-184.

Starr, R. 1987. Clinical judgment of abuse-proneness based upon parent-child interactions. *Child Abuse & Neglect, 11,* 87-92.

Wehrspann, W., Steinhauer, P., & Klajner-Diamond, H. (1987). Criteria and methodology for assessing credibility of sexual abuse allegation. *Canadian Journal of Psychiatry, 32,* 615-623.

2

Interviewer Objectivity and Allegations of Sexual Abuse

The issue of *interviewer objectivity* and what this term exactly means are very important ones. This chapter discusses authors' opinions about whether evaluators should take a believing, neutral, or skeptical stance toward an allegation of sexual abuse; research that has examined the causes and effects of various stances toward sexual abuse; circumstances of the evaluation that might affect interviewer objectivity; and research on false allegations by children.

Review and Critique

A number of authors observed that confirmatory or disconfirmatory bias can affect the outcome of an evaluation (Ney, 1995; Robin, 1991; Yuille, Tymofievich, & Marxen, 1995). The literature reflects a spectrum of opinion regarding evaluator stance.

Sgroi (1980), a pioneer in the sexual abuse field, wrote that "recognition of sexual molestation in a child is entirely dependent on the individual's

inherent willingness to entertain the possibility that the condition may exist"
(pp. 29-30). Herman (1981) and McCarty (1981) take an a priori position that
most accounts are true. Faller (1984, 1988), drawing on clinical experience
and research, asserts that false allegations are quite rare and points out that
children have little motivation for making a false accusation, but offenders
have considerable motivation for persuading professionals that the child is
either lying, mistaken, or "crazy."

In contrast, the AACAP guidelines (1990) advocate "emotional neutrality"
and "an open mind." White and Quinn (1988) argue in favor of a neutral
position, suggesting that any other might contaminate the content of the
interview. Because of this, they recommend that the interviewer have no
information other than the child's name and age (White, Strom, Santilli, &
Halpin, 1986) before interviewing the child. Others have found that background
information facilitates artful and thorough exploration for possible sexual
abuse (Faller, 1988; Morgan, 1995). Myers (1992), in reviewing interviewing practices, states that White and colleagues' argument is "without merit"
(p. 75).

Other authors, for example, Gardner (1992) and Wakefield and Underwager (1988), assert that one should be skeptical of children's statements
about sexual abuse because the vast majority, in general, or in certain contexts
(e.g., divorce, day care) are false. Some who are skeptical hold the opinion
that children frequently make false allegations because of some external
influence, for example, a vindictive accusing parent or an incompetent
"validator" (Gardner, 1992). Others regard the defendant's rights as overrid-
ing and are less concerned with issues of protection of children and society
from sex offenders.

Four studies have examined the effect of interviewer characteristics on
conclusions about sexual abuse (Boat & Everson, 1989; Everson, Boat, &
Robertson, 1992; Jackson & Nuttal, 1993; Kendall-Tackett & Watson, 1991).
The relevant characteristics studied are the respondent's gender, profession,
professional experience, and beliefs about the likelihood of sexual abuse.

The researchers vary somewhat in their approach. Boat and Everson
(1989), in their first study, asked child protective services workers what
proportion of the cases they saw were false allegations and then conducted
follow-up interviews with both those who reported no false allegations and
those who reported false allegations. The second study (Everson et al., 1992)
was somewhat different in that the researchers asked the respondents about
the likelihood that children of different ages and gender would be lying when
reporting sexual abuse. Jackson and Nuttal (1993) used vignettes of possible

sexual abuse, systematically varying race, victim characteristics, offender characteristics, and family characteristics. Kendall-Tackett and Watson (1991) asked professionals, whom they divided into two general categories (law enforcement and mental health personnel), whether they approached an allegation with a believing, neutral, or skeptical stance and then asked them to rate 14 indicators of possible sexual abuse for three different age groups.

On the whole, the research indicates that professionals are likely to believe children when they report sexual abuse. However, there are some variations based on professional and abuse characteristics, and some inconsistencies among studies.

A fairly consistent finding is that women professionals are more likely to make a finding of sexual abuse than men, when presented with either vignettes or behavioral indicators. An exception to this finding is to be noted in Everson et al. (1992), and Boat and Everson (1989) present no data on gender.

Kendall-Tackett and Watson (1991) queried about general stance and predictably found that respondents with a believing stance were more likely to rate the various characteristics presented to them by the researchers as indicative of sexual abuse. Boat and Everson (1989) found that workers reporting false allegations, as compared to those reporting none, were more likely to be skeptical about children's reports.

Generally, legal professionals (law enforcement, judges, attorneys) were more skeptical than were mental health professionals, and Everson and colleagues (1992) found a small but important minority (10%) of judges and law enforcement officers to believe substantial proportions of reports are untrue. In contrast, Kendall-Tackett and Watson (1991) found that law enforcement personnel reported smaller percentages of false accounts than mental health professionals. The former were more persuaded by reenactments with anatomical dolls and by general symptoms, such as depression, aggression, and fear of the perpetrator, than mental health personnel.

Everson and colleagues (1992) found that persons seeing greater numbers of cases were less likely to think children's reports were false. However, Jackson and Nuttal (1993) found younger professionals more likely to believe children in their vignettes had been sexually abused.

Among Boat and Everson's (1989) child protective services sample, 54 (of 88 respondents) reported having investigated no cases where children falsely alleged sexual abuse in the past year. Also, Everson and colleagues (1992) found a certain percentage of respondents believe children "never lie" (judges = 14%; law enforcement = 9%; mental health = 14%; child protective services workers = 30%).

Finally, with regard to victim characteristics, younger children generally were judged more believable than older ones, and Everson and colleagues found boys were more likely to be regarded as truthful. In their earlier study (Boat & Everson, 1989), in more than half the cases one reason cited for believing the allegation false was the child's retraction.

A potential influence on evaluator objectivity is the circumstance under which the evaluation is conducted. Mark Everson (personal communication, 1993) has noted that the relative amount of time the evaluator spends with the child and the alleged offender may influence the opinion. In addition, who is paying for the evaluation and whom the interviewer sees first can affect the evaluator's objectivity, often without conscious awareness. Although nothing has been written directly about a related issue, it is clear from a review of the literature that evaluators who routinely are retained by the accused (e.g., Gardner, 1992; Wakefield & Underwager, 1988) are much more skeptical than those who conduct evaluations for child protective services or law enforcement, for example (e.g., Everson et al., 1992; Faller, 1988; Sgroi, 1982).

Other potential influences are the amount of information about the case and sources of information. For instance, if the evaluator receives volumes of background information related to the victim and nothing about the offender, this may influence the interviewer's stance.

The known facts of the case at hand will also affect the interviewer's stance. For example, if there is a positive finding for venereal disease or evidence of vaginal penetration, the interviewer will likely approach the evaluation with conviction that the child has been sexually abused. On the other hand, if the child has made a false allegation in the past and/or the allegation is vague, greater skepticism will be warranted.

The research on false allegations and the context in which they are likely to be made are relevant here. This research and its limitations will be covered in some detail later in the study guide. However, it suggests that false allegations by children are uncommon, representing between 1% and 10% of reports by children (Berliner, 1988; Faller, 1988; Horowitz, Salt, & Gomes-Schwartz, 1984; Jones & McGraw, 1987). As will be discussed at greater length later, there are certain situations in which the probability may be higher, for example, with older children, with children who have been previously sexually abused, and in divorce situations.

STUDY QUESTIONS

1. Discuss the spectrum of opinion regarding evaluator stance.

   a. What interviewer characteristics seem to be relevant to the interviewer's conclusions about sexual abuse?

   b. What victim characteristics seem to be relevant to the interviewer's conclusions about sexual abuse?

   c. What are some other potential influences on evaluator objectivity?

   d. How does the author suggest we should define an objective evaluator?

To conclude, a consideration of what interviewer objectivity really means must be addressed. An objective evaluator approaches a case with an open mind, but with an appreciation of the research findings on false allegations by children; a recognition of the importance of allowing the facts of the case, as they become known, to determine the evaluator's level of belief or skepticism; and an awareness that the circumstances of the evaluation and the evaluator's personal characteristics can influence her or his reactions to cases in potentially problematic ways (and strategies to guard against an inappropriate stance based on the latter).

References

American Academy of Child and Adolescent Psychiatry (AACAP). (1990, December). *Guidelines for the evaluation of child and adolescent sexual abuse.* (Available from AACAP, 3615 Wisconsin Ave. N.W., Washington, DC 20016)

Berliner, L. (1988). Deciding whether or not the child has been sexually abused. In B. Nicholson & J. Bulkley (Eds.), pp. 48-70. *Allegations of sexual abuse in divorce and custody disputes.* Washington, DC: American Bar Association.

Boat, B., & Everson, M. (1989). False allegations of sexual abuse by children and adolescents. *Journal of the American Academy of Child and Adolescent Psychiatry, 28,* 230-235.

Everson, M., Boat, B., & Robertson, K. (1992, January). *Beliefs about the frequency of false allegations of child sexual abuse: Where you stand depends on where you sit.* Presentation at the conference on the Health Science Response to Child Maltreatment, San Diego, CA. (Available from Mark Everson, Program on Childhood Abuse and Trauma, Department of Psychiatry, CB 7160, University of North Carolina, Chapel Hill, NC 27599-7160)

Faller, K. C. (1984). Is the child victim of sexual abuse telling the truth? *Child Abuse & Neglect, 8,* 473-481.

Faller, K. C. (1988). *Child sexual abuse: An interdisciplinary manual for diagnosis, case management, and treatment.* New York: Columbia University Press.

Gardner, R. (1992). *True and false accusations of child sex abuse.* Cresskill, NJ: Creative Therapeutics.

Herman, J. (1981). *Father-daughter incest.* Cambridge, MA: Harvard University Press.

Horowitz, J., Salt, P., & Gomes-Schwartz, B. (1984). Unconfirmed cases of sexual abuse. In Tufts New England Medical Center, Division of Child Psychiatry, *Sexually exploited children: Service and research* (Unpublished final report). (Available from the Department of Psychiatry, Tufts New England Medical Center, Medford, MA)

Jackson, H., & Nuttal, B. (1993). Clinicians' bias in evaluating allegations of sexual abuse. *Child Abuse & Neglect, 17(1),* 127-144.

Jones, D., & McGraw, E. M. (1987). Reliable and fictitious accounts of sexual abuse to children. *Journal of Interpersonal Violence, 2,* 27-45.

Kendall-Tackett, K., & Watson, M. (1991). Factors that influence professionals' perceptions of behavioral indicators of child sexual abuse. *Journal of Interpersonal Violence, 6,* 385-395.

McCarty, L. (1981). Investigation of incest: Opportunity to motivate families to seek help. *Child Welfare, 60,* 679-689.

Morgan, M., with Edwards, V. (1995). *How to interview sexual abuse victims: Including the use of anatomical dolls.* Thousand Oaks, CA: Sage.

Myers, J. E. B. (1992). *Legal issues in child abuse and neglect.* Newbury Park, CA: Sage.

Ney, T. (Ed.). (1995) *True and false allegations of child sexual abuse.* New York: Brunner/Mazel.

Robin, M. (1991). *Assessing child maltreatment reports: The problem of false allegations.* New York: Haworth.

Sgroi, S. (1980). Sexual molestation of children: The last frontier of child abuse. In L. Schultz (Ed.), *Sexual victimology of youth.* Springfield, IL: Charles C Thomas.

Sgroi, S. (1982). *Handbook of clinical intervention in child sexual abuse.* Lexington, MA: Lexington Books.

Wakefield, H., & Underwager, R. (1988). *Accusations of child sexual abuse.* Springfield, IL: Charles C Thomas.

White, S., & Quinn. K. (1988). Investigatory independence in child sexual abuse evaluations: Conceptual considerations. *Bulletin of the American Academy of Psychiatry and the Law, 16,* 269-278.

White, S., Strom, G., Santilli, G., & Halpin, B. (1986). Interviewing young sexual abuse victims with anatomically correct dolls. *Child Abuse and Neglect, 10,* 510-519.

Yuille, J. Tymofievich, M., & Maxey, D. (1995). The nature of child sexual abuse allegations. In T. Ney (Ed.), *True and false allegations of child sexual abuse,* pp. 21-48. New York: Brunner/Mazel.

Number of Child Interviews

Basic References

American Academy of Child and Adolescent Psychiatry (AACAP). (1990, December). *Guidelines for the evaluation of child and adolescent sexual abuse.*

American Professional Society on the Abuse of Children (APSAC). (1990). *Guidelines for psychosocial evaluation of suspected sexual abuse in young children.*

Morgan, M., with Edwards, V. (1995). *How to interview sexual abuse victims: Including the use of anatomical dolls.* Newbury Park, CA: Sage.

Review and Critique

In considering the number of interviews needed in a case of alleged sexual abuse, a differentiation should be made between multiple interviews by different professionals and several interviews by the same person.

MULTIPLE INTERVIEWS BY DIFFERENT PROFESSIONALS

In a survey of sexual abuse experts, Conte and colleagues (1991) addressed the former issue. They found that, on average, children had talked to 2.3 persons about their sexual abuse before seeing the expert. One concern about this is the potential for contamination of the child's disclosure. In addition, professionals assume, without specific empirical support, that having to repeat a description of sexual victimization to several different people is inherently traumatic, in part because these persons are strangers (Hibbard & Hartmann, 1993; Sgroi, 1982). In addition, some of them may not be supportive. Therefore, a goal in management of sexual abuse cases is to minimize the number of different professionals who interview the child. This goal must be balanced against the needs of different professionals to know about the case and the fact that each of these professionals may require different information from the child. Hibbard and Hartmann (1993) suggest having a multidisciplinary team behind a one-way mirror while a single trained interviewer assesses the child or, alternatively, cross-training professionals so that they can elicit information for more than one discipline.

NUMBER OF INTERVIEWS BY ONE PROFESSIONAL

The appropriate or optimal number of interviews by a single decision maker has been the subject of both writing and discussion. Authors have been concerned about the risks both of too few and too many interviews.

Many of the written guidelines for interviewing children suspected of sexual abuse recommend more than one interview (APSAC, 1990; Faller, 1988; White, Strom, Santilli, & Quinn, n.d.), and in some instances extended evaluations are advocated (Boat & Everson, 1988). Although not necessarily articulated in these writings, there are at least four possible reasons for more than one interview. The evaluator may want to conduct more than one interview before deciding that the child has not been sexually abused (Faller, 1988); before deciding that the child has been sexually abused (White et al., n.d.); before concluding that she or he understands the full extent of sexual abuse (APSAC, 1990); or so that the child's overall functioning and developmental status, as well as possible sexual abuse, can be assessed (APSAC, 1990).

Some clinicians recommend using the first interview to get to know the child and only asking about sexual abuse during the second. Others recommend using the second interview to have the child again describe the abuse to check for consistency (White et al., n.d.).

st two or more interviews in part to allow the
cial assessment, not just a determination of
s recommendation is based on research by
) found that many children initially deny and
ise with a tentative disclosure and therefore
e the abuse is completely understood. Morgan
iews or more, a few days apart, because most
verything in a single interview. Although full
tion planning, it sometimes more properly
ss.

xtended evaluations are recommended when
are inconclusive (Boat & Everson, 1988) and
ige 3 and under (Everson, 1992; Hewitt, 1991).
ldren have short attention spans and limited
tly.

AP guidelines (1990) caution against too many
child be seen the minimum number of times
umber of people necessary" (p. 2). They raise
ews may cause the child unnecessary stress and
he or he has not provided enough information,
ation. In the case of alleged multiple victims
who lived in a ticket [Jordan, Minnesota (Humphrey, 1985), and in
the McMartin preschool case (Wilkinson, Rainey, & staff, 1989), concerns
about the effect of multiple interviews played a role in the failure to convict
alleged offenders.[1]

Nevertheless, the majority of sexual abuse investigations consist of one
interview, and more than one interview is only resorted to when the first
interview is inconclusive. The practice of a single interview is not only
characteristic of child protection investigations but also of some of the
foremost diagnostic programs in the country (Center for Child Protection,
Children's Hospital and Health Center, San Diego, CA, and CARES Program,
Emmanual Hospital, Portland, OR; see Center for Child Protection, 1992;
Guidelines for social work, n.d.). However, the goal of these programs is to
determine whether children have been sexually abused. They generally do
not assess children's overall functioning and do a cursory assessment of
developmental level and competency. Thus, their goals may be more circum-
scribed than programs conducting multiple interviews.

```
┌─────────────────────────────────────────────────────────────┐
│                                                               │
│            S T U D Y   Q U E S T I O N S                      │
│                                                               │
│   Discuss the spectrum of opinion regarding the appropriate   │
│   or optimal number of interviews in evaluating allegations   │
│   of sexual abuse.                                            │
│                                                               │
│   1. What are the four basic reasons for conducting more      │
│      than one interview?                                      │
│                                                               │
│   2. What are the real and perceived risks of too many        │
│      interviews?                                              │
│                                                               │
│   3. What specific issues should the evaluator consider in    │
│      deciding how many interviews are necessary?              │
│                                                               │
└─────────────────────────────────────────────────────────────┘
```

CONCLUSION

In conclusion, in making decisions about the number of interviews necessary, the evaluator should consider several issues. These include the purpose of the assessment/investigation, that is, whether its goal is solely to explore possible sexual abuse or whether overall functioning is also being determined; the functioning and needs of the individual child, including any intentions related to disclosure; the child's age; anxiety and activity level; issues of child safety and support; and practical aspects of conducting the assessment. In addition, interviewers should be sensitive to the risks of too many interviews, both real and perceived.

Note

1. In the Minnesota case, one offender confessed and was sentenced.

References

American Academy of Child and Adolescent Psychiatry (AACAP). (1990, December). *Guidelines for the evaluation of child and adolescent sexual abuse.* (Available from AACAP, 3615 Wisconsin Ave. N.W., Washington, DC 20016)

American Professional Society on the Abuse of Children (APSAC). (1990). *Guidelines for psychosocial evaluation of suspected sexual abuse in young children.* (Available from APSAC, 332 S. Michigan Ave., Chicago, IL 60604)

Boat, B., & Everson, M. (1988). Interviewing young children with anatomical dolls. *Child Welfare, 67*, 336-352.

Campis, L. B., Hebden-Curtis, J., & Demaso, D. R. (1993). Developmental differences in detection and disclosure of sexual abuse. *Journal of the American Academy of Child and Adolescent Psychiatry, 32*, 920-924.

Center for Child Protection. (1992). *Sexual abuse evidentiary protocol.* (Available from Center for Child Protection, Children's Hospital and Health Center, San Diego, CA 92123)

Conte, J., Sorenson, E., Fogarty, L., & Dalla Rosa, J. (1991). Evaluating children's reports of sexual abuse: Results from a survey of professionals. *American Journal of Orthopsychiatry, 61*, 428-437.

Everson, M. (1992). *Guidelines for assessing the very young child.* Unpublished manuscript. (Available from Mark Everson, Program on Childhood Abuse and Trauma, Department of Psychiatry, CB 7160, University of North Carolina, Chapel Hill, NC 27599-7160)

Faller, K. C. (1988). *Child sexual abuse: An interdisciplinary manual for diagnosis, case management, and treatment.* New York: Columbia University Press.

Guidelines for social work interview. (n.d.). Portland, OR: CARES Program, Emmanuel Hospital.

Hewitt, S. (1991). Therapeutic management of preschool cases of alleged but unsubstantiated sexual abuse. *Child Welfare, 70*, 59-67.

Hibbard, R. A., & Hartmann, G. A. (1993). Components of child and parent interviews in cases of alleged sexual abuse. *Child Abuse & Neglect, 17*, 495-500.

Humphrey, H., III. (1985). *Report on Scott County investigations.* Minneapolis: Office of the Attorney General, State of Minnesota.

Morgan, M., with Edwards, V. (1995). *How to interview sexual abuse victims: Including the use of anatomical dolls.* Thousand Oaks, CA: Sage.

Sgroi, S. (1982). *Handbook of clinical intervention in child sexual abuse.* Lexington, MA: Lexington Books.

Sorenson, T., & Snow, B. (1991). How children tell: The process of disclosure in child sexual abuse. *Child Welfare, 70*, 3-15.

Wilkinson, T., Rainey, J., & staff. (1989, January 19). Tapes of the children decided the case for most jurors. *Los Angeles Times*, pp. A1, A22.

White, S., Strom, G., Santilli, G., & Quinn, K. (n.d.). *Guidelines for interviewing preschoolers with sexually anatomically detailed dolls.* Cleveland, OH: Case Western Reserve University School of Medicine.

Documentation

Basic References

Conte et al. (1991). Evaluating children's reports of sexual abuse: Results from a survey of professionals.

In addition to topics already discussed in the study guide, Conte and colleagues ascertain what current practice is among sexual abuse experts regarding recording.

Morgan, M., with Edwards, V. (1995). *How to interview sexual abuse victims: Including the use of anatomical dolls.*

Morgan discusses various methods of documenting interview findings, noting some of the advantages and disadvantages of videotaping.

Myers, J. E. B. (1992). *Legal issues in child abuse and neglect.* Newbury Park, CA: Sage.

Myers's book addresses a range of issues relevant to legal aspects of child maltreatment. This includes a full discussion of the advantages and disadvantages of videotaping child interviews, particularly in cases of sexual abuse.

Review and Critique

It is universally agreed that clinicians interviewing children alleged to have been sexually abused need to employ some method of documentation (AACAP, 1990; APSAC, 1990; Morgan, 1995). Conte and colleagues (1991) queried experts as to what means they used. Almost everyone (94%) made notes, but many used other methods as well. About one third of the respondents videotaped (30%) and/or audiotaped (29%). In addition, 8% had another professional record from behind a one-way mirror, and 14% used a professional as a recorder in the room.

The APSAC guidelines (1990) indicate that at minimum there should be written notes and that the use of video- or audiotapes should be determined by professional preference, logistics, and clinical considerations. Morgan's (1995) position is quite similar. The AACAP guidelines take a stronger position in favor of videotaping, describing its various uses, but note that it may have some disadvantages and risks as well.

The practice of videotaping deserves careful consideration. In the mid-1980s, videotaping child interviews was regarded as a virtual panacea that would address many problems of investigating and litigating child sexual abuse (Colby & Colby, 1987). There were expectations that videotapes would relieve the child of multiple interviews, would persuade offenders to confess, and could be used in lieu of child testimony in court. The majority of states passed laws allowing for the use of videotapes in investigation and litigation (American Bar Association, 1985). Although videotaped interviews in some cases can fulfill all of these expectations, this will by no means always be the case. Moreover, there are unanticipated potential disadvantages of videotapes, specifically, defense's use of the tapes to impeach the victim and to attack the interviewer. Because of the risks of videotaping, some programs that previously videotaped have given up the practice (e.g., National Children's Advocacy Center, Huntsville, AL), and some prosecutors actively oppose videotaping (e.g., Wayne County Sex Crimes Unit, Detroit).

ADVANTAGES OF VIDEOTAPING

Myers (1992) has elaborated the advantages and disadvantages of videotaping. He notes the following advantages: It may decrease the number of interviews or the number of interviewers; it provides complete documentation of what is said by the child and interviewer, which may ensure proper interview techniques and eliminate challenges regarding techniques; it could be used to persuade a disbelieving nonabusive parent of the sexual victimization or the offender to confess or plead; for the victim, it may decrease the probability of recantation, can refresh the child's recollection before going to court, or can substitute for the child's testimony; and an expert witness may view the tape to form an opinion about sexual abuse. The AACAP guidelines also mention that a videotape preserves the child's initial statement (assuming the tape is of the initial statement), and it can be used for interviewer supervision.

Additional advantages are that videotaping demonstrates the evaluator's willingness to allow all information used in arriving at an opinion to be reviewed by others; it provides the evaluator with a complete record from which to draw conclusions; the tape may be used to persuade other professionals (e.g., the police or the prosecutor) of the strength of the case; and a videotape can be much more compelling in capturing and communicating the child's affect during the interview than a written report.

DISADVANTAGES OF VIDEOTAPING

Disadvantages enumerated by Myers include the following: The child can be subject to attack because of minor inconsistencies in the child's account; similarly, because disclosure is often gradual, there may be inconsistencies among videotaped sessions, or only some of the sessions are videotaped and these are not the persuasive ones; the technique of the interviewer may become the focus of attack; videotaping may make the child (or interviewer) uncomfortable; the poor quality of the tape may obscure the data; and tapes may be obtained by persons who have no regard for confidentiality. The AACAP guidelines (1990) are more emphatic on this point, noting that "videos may be shown out of context or fall into the hands of those who have no professional obligations of confidentiality or concern for the child's best interest" (p. 5). The AACAP guidelines also note that a videotape can be used to harass a child on cross-examination.

Additional disadvantages of videotaping are that the act of taping may not merely make the child uncomfortable but actually prevent disclosure, and the existence of a videotape may result in the focus of the case becoming entirely interviewer technique, with little regard to what the child may have disclosed. Furthermore, not only may the evaluator need to spend additional time reviewing tapes in preparation for court, but hours may be spent in court showing the videotape and critiquing or defending the interviewing. Finally, although the AACAP guidelines suggest that the child's statement may be given more credence because it is on videotape, in fact, in court a videotape may be less persuasive than live testimony.

STUDY QUESTION

1. What are the advantages and disadvantages of videotaping child interviews?

GOALS OF THE VIDEOTAPES

If the evaluator determines videotaping will be useful, the reason for videotaping should control the specifics of the videotaping process. In situations where videotapes are to be done so that others can evaluate the data that the evaluator employed in arriving at conclusions, all sessions should be taped. If the videotape is to be used to persuade others, the evaluator may choose not to tape initial sessions. The interviewer gathers information from the child, and then makes a videotaped deposition of the child. If the goal is to use the tape in litigation, the evaluator should consult state statutes regarding the use of videotape in court. Generally, there are requirements for the tape's admissibility. These may include a stipulation about who may be the interviewer (e.g., the prosecutor or a designated child interview specialist); a requirement for a court ruling before a videotape can be substituted for live testimony (e.g., a finding that the child is unavailable to testify); limitations regarding the type of hearings at which a tape can be shown; requirements of notice to all parties (e.g., the defense) so that they can be present for the videotaping; and provisions for cross-examination of the child.

STUDY QUESTION

2. If the evaluator determines that videotaping will be useful, how does she or he determine the specifics of the videotaping process?

INFORMING THE CHILD

Regardless of which method of documentation is employed, the child should be informed about documentation (AACAP, 1990; APSAC, 1990). The evaluator can explain the reason for taking notes, video-, or audiotaping as she or he discusses the purpose of the evaluation. With video- and audiotaping, the equipment can be demonstrated for the child. If the evaluator is using a one-way mirror, it is advisable to introduce the child to the people behind the mirror and explain their function. Explanations and their completeness will need to vary depending on the child's developmental stage and specifics of the case.

S T U D Y   Q U E S T I O N S

3. What forms of documentation are used by clinicians in interviewing children alleged to have been sexually abused?

4. What are the various purposes or goals of documentation?

5. Should the child be informed about documentation? How?

ADDITIONAL DOCUMENTATION

Documentation of the child interview often has purposes beyond providing information related to whether a child has been sexually abused (Lucy Berliner, personal communication, 1992). The child's feelings about the sexual abuse, including attributions of responsibility and impact on sense of self and self-image, affect related to the alleged offender, and relationship with the nonoffending parent, may have a significant influence on case management and treatment decisions and should be included in case recording. Moreover, it is important that the interviewer provide some information, however cursory, related to issues of overall functioning of the child.

References

American Academy of Child and Adolescent Psychiatry (AACAP). (1990, December). *Guidelines for the evaluation of child and adolescent sexual abuse.* (Available from AACAP, 3615 Wisconsin Ave. N.W., Washington, DC 20016)

American Bar Association, Criminal Justice Section. (1985). *Recommendations regarding guidelines for fair treatment of child witnesses in cases where child abuse is alleged*. Washington, DC: American Bar Association.

American Professional Society on the Abuse of Children (APSAC). (1990). *Guidelines for psychosocial evaluation of suspected sexual abuse in young children*. (Available from APSAC, 332 S. Michigan Ave., Chicago, IL 60604)

Colby, I., & Colby, D. (1987). Videotaped interviews in child sexual abuse cases: The Texas example. *Child Welfare, 66*, 25-34.

Conte, J., Sorenson, E., Fogarty, L., & Dalla Rosa, J. (1991). Evaluating children's reports of sexual abuse: Results from a survey of professionals. *American Journal of Orthopsychiatry, 61*, 428-437.

Morgan, M., with Edwards, V. (1995). *How to interview sexual abuse victims: Including the use of anatomical dolls*. Thousand Oaks, CA: Sage.

Myers, J. E. B. (1992). *Legal issues in child abuse and neglect*. Newbury Park, CA: Sage.

Standardized Tests

Basic Reference

Friedrich, W. (1990). *Psychotherapy of sexually abused children and their families.* New York: Norton.

Friedrich is the researcher/clinician who has played a pioneering role in using and developing standardized measures that differentiate sexually abused children from those not reported for sexual abuse. His book includes a description of this research and its practical applications.

Review and Critique

Psychological tests are neither necessary nor sufficient for deciding whether a child has been sexually abused. Conte and colleagues (1991) found that only 28% of the experts in their study employ psychological tests during the course of evaluations. However, testing can be helpful as one piece of information to be used to determine whether a child has been sexually victimized and often provides a picture of a child's overall functioning (AACAP, 1990; APSAC, 1990).

Standardized instruments have been employed by researchers as well as by clinicians. Objective measures have been used by both clinicians and researchers, but projective tests have been employed primarily by clinicians. The projective tests are, of course, always completed by the alleged victim, but the objective measures may be given to the children, their caretakers, or their teachers. The vast majority of these instruments are not specific to assessment of sexual abuse, but there is an emerging body of measures for evaluating sexually abused children.

Instruments are chosen for use or developed based on hypotheses regarding the sequelae of sexual abuse. For example, based on a hypothesis that sexual abuse has a negative effect on self-esteem, researchers have employed the Piers Harris Self-Concept Scale (Cohen & Mannarino, 1988; Gomes-Schwartz, Horowitz, & Cardarelli, 1990; Tufts New England Medical Center, 1984). A comparable hypothesis has led to the use of the Children's Depression Inventory with sexually abused children (Cohen & Mannarino, 1988; Lipovsky, Saunders, & Murphy, 1989). Results from research comparing children found to have been sexually abused and nonabused children using these general measures have been mixed (Waterman & Lusk, 1993).

Alleged victims may also be administered intelligence tests, not because of any relationship between intelligence and risk, but to assess some aspects of competency. Research examining the cognitive functioning of sexually abused children fails to find global deficits (Waterman & Lusk, 1993).

STUDY QUESTION

1. How can standardized tests be helpful in child sexual abuse evaluations?

The discussion here will focus on behavioral assessment schedules and projective measures.

Behavior Checklists

A number of behavior checklists, which assess overall functioning and specific symptoms, have been employed with maltreated children, for example, the Louisville Behavior Checklist (Chantler, Pelco, & Mertin, 1993; Tufts New England Medical Center, 1984) and the Achenbach Child Behavior Checklist (CBCL; Einbender & Friedrich, 1989; Friedrich, 1990; Friedrich, Beilke, & Urquiza, 1988). Chantler and colleagues (1993) found limited support for the utility of the Louisville Behavior Checklist in differentiating a sexually abused sample, a clinical sample, and a community sample. The CBCL is the most widely used, with both sexually and otherwise maltreated children. Waterman and Lusk (1993) report 11 studies in which sexually abused and nonabused children were compared. The CBCL can be used with children, ages 2 through 16, and has versions that are completed by the child, the caretaker, and the teacher. Studies suggest that sexually abused children have more behavior problems than nonabused children, but not more than other clinician samples. In addition, sexually abused children score significantly higher on the sexual problems subscale of the CBCL (Waterman & Lusk, 1993).

The researcher/clinician who has done the most work with the CBCL comparing responses of children alleged to have been sexually abused to other clinical populations is William Friedrich, a member of the APSAC Board of Directors, at the Mayo Clinic. However, Friedrich (1990) reasoned that a key marker of sexually abused children was sexualized behavior, and the CBCL and comparable instruments have only a small number of items related to sexualized behavior.

Accordingly, he developed a checklist especially for measuring symptoms that tend to be specific to sexually victimized children, the Child Sexual Behavior Inventory (CSBI; Friedrich, 1990). Version 2 has 36 items and has been shown to reliably discriminate between children alleged to have been sexually abused and allegedly nonabused children, with a sample of 260 sexually victimized children and 880 nonabused children (Friedrich, 1990). A third version is presently being field tested (Friedrich, 1995).

However, it is important to appreciate that some victims are nonsymptomatic, so that the absence of a pathological level of sexualized behavior does not mean the child has not been sexually abused. Friedrich (1994) has observed that sexualized behavior is the most frequently found marker of sexual abuse, but nevertheless is present in only about 40% of the children believed to have been sexually abused. In addition, a limitation of this instrument, and others that rely on caretaker report, is that caretakers may be biased. For example, if they are in denial regarding the sexual abuse, they may minimize the sexualized behavior. Conversely, a parent who is overwhelmed by discovering the sexual abuse may overreport sexualized behavior. This limitation is addressed in version 3.

Another checklist specific to sexual abuse is the Sexual Abuse Symptom Checklist (Kolko, Moser, & Weldy, 1988), which holds promise but has been less extensively tested than the CSBI. Responses of 29 sexually abused children were compared to those of 52 physically abused children. The checklist was found to reliably discriminate between the two groups (Kolko et al., 1988).

Yet another instrument that is intended to address the dearth of instruments specific to sexually abused (and other traumatized) children is the Trauma Symptom Checklist for Children (TSC-C; Briere, 1989; Briere & Lanktree, 1992). The TSC-C is designed for children age 8 and older and has six subscales (anxiety, depression, posttraumatic stress, sexual concerns, dissociation, and anger). It has been shown to be psychometrically reliable and to have predictive validity (Briere, in press).

In a recent study conducted by Elliott and Briere (1994), 399 participants ages 8 to 15 who presented for assessment of possible sexual abuse were compared on a number of measures, including the TSC-C. Based on all measures, the children were classified according to the likelihood of sexual abuse. The children who disclosed some or all of their sexual abuse and who were classified as credible scored the highest overall (most symptomatic) on the six subscales of the TSC-C. The children thought not to have been sexually victimized scored next highest on the TSC-C, and those who were thought to have been sexually abused but who were either not disclosing or recanting scored the lowest on symptoms.

PROJECTIVE TESTS

Clinicians have employed projective measures with the belief that victims will provide content in response to these instruments related to their sexual experiences. The Rorschach, the Children's Apperception Test, the Thematic Apperception Test, and the Roberts Apperception Test have all been used. Friedrich (1990) reports that of these instruments, he prefers the Roberts because the drawings are more active and realistic; furthermore, he points out that Card 15 pulls specifically for sexual themes.

As well, there is a recently developed projective instrument, the Projective Story Telling Cards (PST Cards) especially for the diagnosis and treatment of sexual abuse, other types of maltreatment, and child and family problems (Caruso, 1988). Eight cards are focused specifically on possible sexual abuse. This instrument is the work of a clinical psychologist and an artist colleague. Friedrich (1994) used two of the cards with children having a history of possible sexual abuse and those with no such history. He found that the cards elicited stories involving sexual themes from the vast majority of respondents, and there was no significant difference in the proportion producing such stories between the two groups. Moreover, although the children in the cards are drawn so that they could be of either gender—making the cards useful with both male and female victims—there are few pictures suggesting female sex offenders.

The reader is also cautioned against the use of a later series of PST Cards produced by Casebeer (1989), which depict sexual exploitation and ritual abuse of children. These cards are much more explicit than the earlier cards. For example, several persons in the exploitation cards are partially naked, and ritual abuse cards have graphic representations of satanic acts and artifacts. Although it might be argued that children without exploitation or ritual experiences would not know what these cards portray, the cards may be leading. Moreover, even if they are not, because they are very likely to be so perceived, their use may complicate or prevent needed intervention.

Nevertheless, the 1988 PST Cards, which show scenes of possible sexual abuse, may be useful for sexual abuse assessments. Clinically, if sexual themes are found in the child's responses, they can reinforce the child's statements about sexual abuse; they can reinforce impressions of victimization drawn from other information; or the child's stories can become the springboard for questions about whether the things the child is relating ever happened to her or him.

STUDY QUESTIONS

2. Describe the spectrum of standardized measures that have been employed in sexual abuse evaluations.

   a. Which behavior checklists have been used in assessing maltreated children? Which, in particular, seem to best measure symptoms more specific to sexually abused children?

   b. Which projective tests have been used in assessing maltreated children? Which, in particular, might be helpful in assessing sexual abuse?

   c. What are some specific limitations of behavior checklists in the assessment of child sexual abuse? What are the limitations of projective tests?

References

American Academy of Child and Adolescent Psychiatry (AACAP). (1990, December). *Guidelines for the evaluation of child and adolescent sexual abuse.* (Available from AACAP, 3615 Wisconsin Ave. N.W., Washington, DC 20016)

American Professional Society on the Abuse of Children (APSAC). (1990). *Guidelines for psychosocial evaluation of suspected sexual abuse in young children.* (Available from APSAC, 332 S. Michigan Ave., Chicago, IL 60604)

Briere, J. (1989). *The Trauma Symptom Checklist for Children.* Unpublished instrument. (Available from John Briere, Department of Psychiatry, University of Southern California, Los Angeles, CA)

Briere, J. (in press). *Professional manual for the Trauma Symptom Checklist.* Odessa, FL: Psychological Assessment Resources.

Briere, J., & Lanktree, C. (1992, January). *Further data on the Trauma Symptom Checklist for Children: Reliability, validity, and sensitivity to treatment.* Paper presented at the Conference on Responding to Child Maltreatment, San Diego, CA.

Caruso, K. (1988). *Basic users manual to accompany Projective Story Telling Cards.* Redding, CA: Northwest Psychological.

Casebeer, M. (1989). *Projective Story Telling Cards.* Redding, CA: Northwest Psychological.

Chantler, L., Pelco, L., & Mertin, P. (1993). The psychological evaluation of child sexual abuse using the Louisville Behavior Checklist and human figure drawing. *Child Abuse & Neglect, 17,* 271-279.

Cohen, J., & Mannarino, A. (1988). Psychological symptoms of sexually abused girls. *Child Abuse & Neglect, 12,* 571-577.

Conte, J., Sorenson, E., Fogarty, L., & Dalla Rosa, J. (1991). Evaluating children's reports of sexual abuse: Results from a survey of professionals. *American Journal of Orthopsychiatry, 61,* 428-437.

Einbender, A., & Friedrich, W. (1989). Psychological functioning and behavior of sexually abused girls. *Journal of Consulting and Clinical Psychology, 57,* 155-157.

Elliott, D., & Briere, J. (1994, January). Forensic sexual abuse evaluations of older children: Disclosures and symptomology. *Behavioral Sciences and the Law, 12,* 261-277.

Friedrich, W. (1990). *Psychotherapy of sexually abused children and their families.* New York: Norton.

Friedrich, W. (1994, January). *APSAC Institute: Treatment outcomes in child sexual abuse.* Paper presented at the Conference on Responding to Child Maltreatment, Center for Child Protection, Children's Hospital and Health Center, San Diego, CA.

Friedrich, W. (1995, July). *Sexual behavior in sexually abused children.* Paper presented at the 4th International Family Violence Research Conference, New England Center, Durham, NH.

Friedrich, W., Beilke, R., & Urquiza, A. (1988). Behavior problems in young sexually abused boys: A comparison study. *Journal of Interpersonal Violence, 3*, 21-28.

Gomes-Schwartz, B., Horowitz, J. M., & Cardarelli, A. P. (Eds.). (1990). *Child sexual abuse: The initial effects.* Newbury Park, CA: Sage.

Kolko, D., Moser, J., & Weldy, S. (1988). Behavioral/emotional indicators of sexual abuse in child psychiatric inpatients: A controlled comparison with physical abuse. *Child Abuse & Neglect, 12*, 529-541.

Lipovsky, J., Saunders, B., & Murphy, S. (1989). Depression, anxiety, and behavior problems among victims of father-child sexual assault and nonabused siblings. *Journal of Interpersonal Violence, 4*, 452-468.

Tufts New England Medical Center, Division of Child Psychiatry. (1984). *Sexually exploited children: Service and research project* (Final report for the Office of Juvenile Justice and Delinquency Prevention). Washington, DC: U.S. Department of Justice.

Waterman, J., & Lusk, R. (1993). Psychological testing in evaluation of child sexual abuse. *Child Abuse & Neglect, 17*, 145-159.

Questioning Techniques

Review and Critique

The APSAC guidelines (1990) and many clinicians (e.g., Benedek & Schetky, 1987a, 1987b; Morgan, 1995) have admonished interviewers to avoid the use of leading questions when assessing for possible sexual abuse. However, rarely do they define or give examples of leading questions.

The research that has been done on leading questions consists of analogue studies, that is, naturally occurring or staged events that children are then asked to describe. The interviewer uses a variety of questions, including those that are direct, leading, misleading, and suggestive. This research will be discussed in some detail in the section on children as witnesses. However, with the exception of one study (Bruck, Ceci, Francoueur, & Renick, 1994), it indicates that children generally are resistant to leading questions but many are susceptible to programming and coercive interrogations.

Several authors have proposed guidelines for questioning based on clinical experience and/or common sense (Boat & Everson, 1988; Boychuk & Stellar, 1992; Center for Child Protection, 1992; Faller, 1993; Morgan, 1995; Myers, 1992; White & Quinn, 1988). There is a slight disjuncture between these research findings and the clinical writings, in that clinicians generally advise interviewers to be more conservative than the research suggests they need be. This advice is in part based on legal considerations.

White and Quinn (1988) take the most conservative position. Although acknowledging that their concerns are not based on research, they advise against the use of questions to which the response is either yes or no and against the use of multiple-choice questions, defining both types of questions as leading. Morgan (1995) makes similar points, but also says that sometimes these questions are necessary to elicit needed information.

Moreover, White and Quinn and others (e.g., Benedek & Schetky, 1987a, 1987b) state that interviewers engage in coercive questioning techniques such as admonishing the child, with various degrees of forcefulness, to tell the truth; offering tangible rewards; repetitive questioning; threats; and setting limits, such as telling the child she or he cannot leave the interview to go to the bathroom until the child discloses. Although there is no evidence that such techniques are widespread, they have no place in child interviews.

Others (Boat & Everson, 1988; Boychuk & Stellar, 1992; Faller, 1990, 1993; Myers, 1992; Stellar & Boychuk, 1992) advise the interviewer to be very self-conscious about questions, to employ more open-ended questions before resorting to more close-ended ones, and to appreciate that responses to close-ended questions may be less accurate. More close-ended questions may also result in challenges to the admissibility of findings in court (Charles Wilson, personal communication, 1992).

RECOMMENDATIONS FROM VARIOUS WRITERS

Faller proposes a continuum of questions from open-ended to close-ended, suggesting the interviewer should have more confidence in the child's responses to the open-ended questions. She advises a strategy that employs the most open-ended questions that elicit information, resorting to more close-ended ones only when open-ended ones are unproductive, and reverting to more open-ended questions once new information is given by the child. The continuum she suggests begins with general questions, such as "Do you know why you are here today?" followed by focused questions, which may focus on the person who may have abused the child ("Tell me about what you do with your daddy." "Is there anything your daddy does that you don't like?"), the private parts of the body ("Did you ever see a man's peepee?" "When was that?"), or the possible circumstances of the abuse ("What do you do when grandpa baby-sits?"), then multiple-choice questions, yes-no questions, and finally leading questions (questions for which the desired response is obvious—"Daddy put his finger in your peepee, didn't he?").

Although Faller thinks that multiple-choice questions are acceptable if, for example, the child says, "I don't remember" to a focused question, she admonishes the interviewer to be sure a correct response is included in the choices. She also suggests that such questions be limited to queries about the context of possible abuse and not be employed to query about abusive acts themselves. As noted already, White and Quinn (1988) oppose the use of multiple-choice questions; so does Morgan (1995). Faller cautions that yes-no questions may result in social-desirability responses and asserts that leading questions have no place in sexual abuse evaluations.

Myers's (1992) continuum appears to draw on the work of both Faller and White and Quinn. He proposes a continuum beginning with open-ended, followed by focused, then leading, and finally coercive, questions. In addition, he argues that focused and leading questions vary in the degree of their suggestiveness.

Boat and Everson (1988), writing about the use of anatomical dolls, differentiate among the three types of focused questions specified by Faller, defining those related to circumstances (critical events focus) as the most open-ended, followed by person focused (critical individuals focus), and body parts questions (direct general inquiry), as the most close-ended. As well, they state that yes-no questions (direct inquiry about specific individuals—"Has daddy ever touched your dingdong?") are potentially leading and suggestive, especially with 2- and 3-year-olds, who may give affirmative responses when they do not understand the question. Yes-no questions should only be used when there is good cause for concern about sexual abuse, but no disclosure. In such instances, they can be effective in "opening the door" and facilitating disclosure.

Boychuk and Stellar (1992; Stellar & Boychuk, 1992) recommend first trying to elicit a free narrative from the child, using directives such as "I heard something may have happened to you." When the child is talking, she or he should not be interrupted. However, open-ended questions should be used to clarify information from the narrative or to direct the child to a specific incident. They believe focusing on the last time the child was abused or a novel time is the best way to tap episodic memory. In addition, they suggest the use of cue questions, which rely on one or two words from the background information. These may be helpful after the free narrative to gather additional detail, or when other types of questioning have not elicited any information. Finally, direct questions may be appropriate as a last resort. These are defined as questions probing for information about "who," "what," and "where." If the child provides a response to a direct question, the child is then asked to provide a narrative.

The *Sexual Abuse Evidentiary Protocol* from the Center for Child Protection (1992) also advises using focused, but not leading, questions. However, they ask about a full range of sexual activity: oral contact; digital contact; vaginal, penile, and anal contact, as well as pornography, something not specifically recommended by other authors. The protocol advises phrasing the question as "Was there any touching with mouths?" rather than "Did his mouth touch your peepee?" in order not to lead the child. As well, the protocol advises using multiple-choice questions to inquire about the identity of the offender, rather than asking directly whether it was, for example, the father.

Reed (1993) suggests preparing the child before questioning to be autonomous in responding. He does this by encouraging the child to disagree, to admit lack of memory, to admit confusion, and to decline to answer a question that is too hard.

STUDY QUESTIONS

1. Generally, how do children seem to respond to leading questions?
2. Discuss the spectrum of proposed guidelines for questioning children. What type(s) of questions does each writer define as leading questions?
   a. What strategy is advised by Faller? Describe her proposed continuum of questions.
   b. When, and only when, should yes-no questions be used?
   c. How does Faller define appropriate practice?

CONCLUSION

It is apparent from the discussion that authors generally agree about the importance of using questions as open-ended as possible. However, their typologies of questions vary somewhat, as do their opinions about how leading particular types of questions may be. Evaluators are engaging in appropriate practice if they adopt any of these typologies or adapt one or more to their needs. However, interviewers should avoid questions that are too leading.

References

American Professional Society on the Abuse of Children (APSAC). (1990). *Guidelines for psychosocial evaluation of suspected sexual abuse in young children.* (Available from APSAC, 332 S. Michigan Ave., Chicago, IL 60604)

Benedek, E., & Schetky, D. (1987a). Problems in validating allegations of sexual abuse: Part 1. Factors affecting perception and recall of events. *Journal of the American Academy of Child and Adolescent Psychiatry, 26,* 912-915.

Benedek, E., & Schetky, D. (1987b). Problems in validating allegations of sexual abuse: Part 2. Clinical evaluation. *Journal of the American Academy of Child and Adolescent Psychiatry, 26,* 916-921.

Boat, B., & Everson, M. (1988). Interviewing young children with anatomical dolls. *Child Welfare, 67,* 337-352.

Boychuk, T., & Stellar, M. (1992). *Videotaped forensic interview of the school age child.* Unpublished manuscript. (Available from Tascha Boychuk, Center for Child Protection, St. Joseph's Hospital, Phoenix, AZ)

Bruck, M., Ceci, S., Francoueur, E., & Renick, A. (1994). *Anatomically detailed dolls do not facilitate preschoolers' reports of a pediatric examination involving genital touching.* Unpublished manuscript. (Available from Maggie Bruck, Psychology Department, McGill University, 1205 Docteur Penfield Ave., Montreal, Quebec, Canada H3A 1B1)

Center for Child Protection. (1992). *Sexual abuse evidentiary protocol.* (Available from the Center for Child Protection, Children's Hospital and Health Center, San Diego, CA 92123)

Faller, K. C. (1990, Spring). Types of questions for assessing allegation of sexual abuse. *APSAC Advisor, 3*(2), 5-7.

Faller, K. C. (1993). *Child sexual abuse: Assessment and intervention issues.* Washington, DC: U.S. Department of Health and Human Services, National Center on Child Abuse and Neglect.

Morgan, M., with Edwards, V. (1995). *How to interview sexual abuse victims: Including the use of anatomical dolls.* Thousand Oaks, CA: Sage.

Myers, J. E. B. (1992). *Legal issues in child abuse and neglect.* Newbury Park, CA: Sage.

Reed, D. (1993). Enhancing children's resistance to misleading questions in forenic interviews. *APSAC Advisor, 6*(2), 3-8.

Stellar, M., & Boychuk, T. (1992). Children as witnesses in sexual abuse cases: Investigative interview and assessment techniques. In H. Dent & R. Flin (Eds.), *Children as witnesses* (pp. 47-71). West Sussex, UK: Wiley.

White, S., & Quinn, K. (1988). Investigatory independence in child sexual abuse evaluations: Conceptual considerations. *Bulletin of the American Academy of Psychiatry and the Law, 16,* 269-278.

Media for Interviewing Children

Interviewing a child alleged to have been sexually abused rarely involves just talking, nor should it. Generally, additional media are employed because of the belief they may facilitate the child's ability to disclose if something has occurred; because they may allow the interviewer to obtain more and more specific information; and because they may reduce the likelihood of trauma from the interview (Faller, 1993).

Clinicians use a considerable variety of media; however, this discussion will be limited to those most widely used and specific to the assessment of sexual abuse. Anatomical dolls, anatomical drawings, and picture drawing will be described.

Basic References: Anatomical Dolls

**American Professional Society on the Abuse of Children (APSAC).
1990.** *Guidelines for the use of anatomical dolls during investigative
interviews of children who may have been sexually abused.*

These recently published guidelines incorporate research and make suggestions for best practices for using anatomical dolls in investigative interviews.

Faller, K. C. (1993). *Child sexual abuse: Assessment and intervention issues.* Washington, DC: National Center on Child Abuse and Neglect.

This work was prepared for the National Center on Child Abuse and Neglect (NCCAN) for national distribution. Although written by Faller, it was edited by an NCCAN consultant and was subjected to external review by other experts in child sexual abuse. Thus, it represents current professional practice and opinion and is endorsed by NCCAN.

Everson, M., & Boat, B. (1994). Putting the anatomical doll controversy in perspective: An examination of the major uses and criticisms of the dolls in child sexual abuse evaluations. *Child Abuse & Neglect, 18,* 113-130.

Everson and Boat review guidelines for use of anatomical dolls and address the major criticisms of the dolls in light of the functions guidelines advise.

Review and Critique

According to the research of Conte and colleagues (1991), anatomical dolls are the most widely used medium (by 92% of respondents) in interviewing children suspected of being sexually abused. Similarly, Kendall-Tackett and Watson (1991) report that in a survey of 201 Boston area professionals conducting sexual abuse investigations, 80% of mental health professionals and 62% of law enforcement personnel indicated that they employ anatomical dolls. In addition, of the various media employed by evaluators, only the anatomical dolls have been subjected to extensive research. To a considerable extent, this research has been driven by attacks on the dolls in legal arenas. Legal challenges include that they are being improperly employed as a psychological test, that they have grotesquely exaggerated sexual organs, and that they are leading or suggestive. Yet, most of the research supports their efficacy in sexual abuse evaluations (Maan, 1991).

This section will cover the issue of the suggestibility of the dolls, the research on differences in responses of sexually abused and nonabused children to the dolls, the research comparing the effectiveness of anatomical dolls to other techniques, and techniques for using the dolls.

STUDY QUESTIONS

1. How are additional media helpful in interviewing children who allegedly have been sexually abused?
2. Which three media are most widely used in the assessment of sexual abuse? Of these three, which is the most commonly used?

ARE THE DOLLS SUGGESTIVE?

The research on the suggestiveness of the dolls consists of studies of the reactions of children with no history of sexual abuse to the dolls and a study by Bays (1990) of the size of the genitalia and breasts of anatomical dolls.

Most of the research on the reactions of nonabused children to the dolls indicates that the dolls do not elicit sexual activity in the doll play of children with no prior sexual knowledge. However, children may be curious about the sexual parts of the dolls and insert fingers in the orifices.

Sivan, Schor, Koeppl, and Noble (1988) exposed 144 middle-class 3- to 8-year-olds from the Iowa City area to anatomical dolls. None of the children engaged in sexualized behavior with the dolls, only 2% of participants exhibited aggressive play with the dolls, and predictably girls were more interested in the dolls than boys. A more recent study (Dawson, Vaughan, & Wagner, 1992) with a smaller number of children (10 boys and 10 girls) reports comparable findings, with no intercourse behavior demonstrated by the children, but higher percentages engaging in aggressive behavior.

The sample of 223 children involved in a similar study by Everson and Boat (1990; Boat & Everson 1994) was more varied demographically and consisted of younger children from 2 to 5 years old. In addition, in this study children were given the instruction, "Show me what the dolls can do together" after the dolls were undressed. Of the participants, 6% engaged the dolls in oral or genital intercourse. None of the 2-year-olds demonstrated such behavior; however, older, black, and poor children had higher rates. The rates for older, black, poor males were 27% (4 of 15) with the interviewer present and 22% (2 of 9) when the child was alone. Only this group demonstrated sexualized behavior with the dolls in the presence of the interviewer. Everson and Boat interviewed the mothers of the children who demonstrated sexualized behavior and found most of them could offer relatively benign explanations for their children's sexual knowledge, usually having viewed pornography or adolescents involved in sexual activity.

In addition, Everson and Boat (1990) also reviewed seven previous studies of children's sexualized behavior with anatomical dolls and noted that the overall rate from these studies is 2%. They conclude, based on their own research and that of others, that the dolls do not cause sexually naive children to act out sexually, but they do appear to provide sexually knowledgeable children a stimulus to engage in sexualized doll play.

In contrast, Bruck et al. (1994) present findings from an analogue study with 3-year-old boys and girls who received medical exams, which they interpret as indicating anatomical dolls are suggestive. Bruck and colleagues found that some children (they do not say how many) inserted fingers in the vaginal and anal openings of the anatomical dolls. Although this behavior is considered normal by clinicians and other researchers, it is judged by these researchers as likely to be viewed by clinicians as suspicious of sexual abuse.

As stated earlier, an additional criticism made of the anatomical dolls is that their enlarged genitals are both traumatic to interviewees and suggestive. Frustrated by these challenges, Bays (1990) set out to study genitalia with 17 adult male dolls and genitalia and breasts of 17 adult female dolls. As well, she reports on a preliminary study of nine pairs of male and female child dolls. Her findings are that the breasts and genitalia of adult dolls are either proportional or smaller than normal (with some penises it depends on whether they are considered stretched or unstretched flaccid penises). With the child dolls, the vulvar openings were proportional to girls ages 4 to 10 and the penises proportional for boys ages 4 to 18. Bays admonishes doll manufacturers that they should make their juvenile penises the equivalent of those for boys ages 3 through 12.

STUDY QUESTIONS

3. What does research on the reactions of nonabused children to anatomical dolls indicate about the suggestiveness of the dolls?
4. What did Bays find in her study of the genitalia of anatomical dolls?

DO SEXUALLY ABUSED CHILDREN REACT DIFFERENTLY TO THE DOLLS THAN NONABUSED CHILDREN?

Four studies compare the responses of children referred for sexual abuse to anatomical dolls to those not so referred. Altogether, 172 children were involved in these four studies; Cohn's (1991) study had the largest number of children, 70. Thus, only a modest number of participants have been involved in this sort of research. All studies had equal numbers of children referred for sexual abuse and nonreferred children, and ages ranged from 2 to 8 years. Except for the research of August and Foreman (1989), who only examined girls, the studies had both male and female participants. With the exception of the research of Cohn, studies found statistically significant and higher proportions of intercourse demonstration by children referred for sexual abuse evaluation. Cohn reports 3% of participants in both groups demonstrated intercourse with the dolls; however, the total exposure time of her children to the dolls was 11 minutes. In all research, a substantial number of the children referred for sexual abuse did not demonstrate sexualized behavior with the dolls; the smallest number (10%) was found in the work of Jampole and Webber (1987), but their study consisted of only 10 children in each group. White et al. (1986) and August and Foreman (1989) report no sexual intercourse demonstrations among their nonreferred participants.

Thus, it appears that sexually abused children are more likely to engage in sexualized behavior with anatomical dolls than are nonabused children. However, many abused children will not demonstrate sexual activity, and a small number of nonabused children will.

STUDY QUESTION

5. What has research demonstrated regarding the different responses of abused and nonabused children to the dolls?

IS THE USE OF ANATOMICAL DOLLS SUPERIOR TO OTHER TECHNIQUES?

Clinicians have felt that using anatomical dolls greatly enhances their ability to elicit information about sexual abuse; however, the research findings, so far, are not as supportive as clinicians might anticipate. There are five studies reporting on the use of anatomical dolls compared to other techniques. Two involve children alleged to have been sexually abused (Britton & O'Keefe, 1991; Leventhal, Hamilton, Rekedal, Tebano-Micci, & Eyster, 1989); one involves research on children seen in an outpatient clinic, including children alleged to have been abused (Steward, 1989); and two are analogue studies (Goodman & Aman, 1990; Bruck et al., 1994). With the exception of the study by Bruck and colleagues (1994), these studies indicate that, generally, using anatomical dolls improves children's responses to abuse-related queries when compared to questioning without props (Goodman & Aman, 1990; Leventhal et al., 1989; Steward, 1989) but that they are not superior to nonanatomical dolls (Goodman & Aman, 1990; Britton & O'Keefe, 1991) or other media (Steward, 1989).

S T U D Y   Q U E S T I O N S

6. What is known about the relative usefulness of anatomical dolls?

7. Describe the one study that does not support the general efficacy of the anatomical dolls.

It is difficult to reconcile the findings of Bruck and colleagues (1994) with other research, because their methodology differs somewhat and their results diverge from those of other doll studies. They found very high rates of inaccuracy among 3-year-olds interviewed within minutes of a medical exam, regardless of method of questioning. Forty children received a well-child exam, during which half received a light touch on the genitals and buttocks. First, the children were asked a direct question about genital and anal touch with anatomical dolls ("Did Dr. F touch you here?" as the interviewer pointed to a private body part). Then they were asked a leading or misleading (misleading if no such touch had occurred) question, "Show on the doll how Dr. F touched your buttocks" (the child's name for the relevant body part was used). Finally, they were commanded to show on their own bodies how Dr. F touched their private parts (this technique was only used with children who had actually experienced the touch). The children provided high rates of false negative responses (about 50%) to these direct questions and commands, and the girls' answers gave high rates of false positives (about 50%) in all three conditions. The response was scored incorrect if the child touched, for example, the anus instead of the vagina in response to a command to show on the doll or themselves how the doctor touched the vagina. In addition, apparently to support their hypothesis that the anatomical dolls are not useful, they recoded behaviors with dolls, departing from their original definition of a correct response. Thus, initially any demonstration of touching, rubbing, or insertion to the correct private part was considered an acceptable response to the command, "Show me on the doll how Dr. F touched your vagina/buttocks." However, because Dr. F only lightly touched the relevant body part, anything other than that was recoded a false positive. As a result, the correct replies for the 3-year-old girls who received the private-parts exam decreased from 71% to 38%.

These findings do not indicate that using anatomical dolls creates inaccuracies but that either the study design (perhaps using a light touch of private parts, when presumably many other parts of the body were handled) is problematic or the young age of the study population led to these somewhat anomalous results. Such high proportions of incorrect responses are not found in other studies, even those involving 3-year-olds. Replication at another site is needed to give weight to the findings (Mark Everson, personal communication, December 1994). This study will be discussed again in the section of the study guide on children's memory and suggestibility.

STRATEGIES FOR USING THE DOLLS

Many authors warn that anatomical dolls should not be used by persons who are untrained in their use (APSAC, 1995; Ney, 1995; Robin, 1991). However, the doll research has not addressed the issue of optimal methods for using them. Therefore, guidelines for their use are based on clinical experience, in some cases, a consensus of a group of professionals, for example, the ASPAC Guidelines (1995) on the use of the dolls.

Everson and Boat (1994) found 20 sets of guidelines for using anatomical dolls. From these, they derived seven different functions for the dolls. The functions and the number of adherents are as follows: (a) a comforter (2), (b) an icebreaker (5), (c) an anatomical model (16), (d) a demonstration aid (18), (e) a memory stimulus (11), (f) a diagnostic screen (11), and (g) a diagnostic test (1 possible).

Their survey demonstrates that views among professionals about how to use the dolls are diverse. However, there is fairly wide support for their use as an anatomical model, that is, as a vehicle for discussing body parts and identifying the child's names for the private parts, and as a demonstration aid, a medium for assisting the child in disclosure of sexual abuse. As noted above, there is limited research that indicates that the dolls (and other props) can facilitate disclosure of private-part touching.

In addition, there is agreement that the use of the dolls is not a psychological test, any more than, for example, using the dollhouse is. Thus, the reaction of children to the dolls cannot be used to categorically differentiate sexually abused from nonabused children. The fact that children fail to demonstrate sexual activity with the dolls does not mean they have not been sexually abused, and conversely, the fact that they do show sexual activity does not mean that they have been sexually abused.

However, a substantial number of authors advocate the use of the dolls as a diagnostic screen. That is, a child's demonstration of sexualized behavior with the dolls raises a concern about sexual abuse, but, by itself, is usually not conclusive. Support for the use of the dolls as a diagnostic screen is found in the research comparing the reactions to the dolls by children alleged to have been sexually abused and those not alleged. Nevertheless, that children's reactions should serve only as a screen is supported by the findings of Everson and Boat's research that nonabused, but sexually knowledgeable, children will be stimulated by the dolls to engage them in sexualized behavior.

Many guidelines see the function of the dolls as a memory stimulus to be important. That is, the sight of the private parts on the dolls jogs the child's memory and may result in a statement or demonstration that provides information about sexual activity. The research cited earlier comparing the effectiveness of anatomical dolls (or other aids) to mere questioning supports their use as a memory stimulus.

STUDY QUESTIONS

8. What are the seven functions for anatomical dolls, as identified by Everson and Boat?

9. Which two functions are generally supported by professionals?

10. Which function is generally unsupported?

In part because guidelines may differ regarding what they describe as the dolls' primary functions, they differ in how they recommend the dolls be used. For example, authors differ in their advice about when the dolls should be presented. Some (Boat & Everson, 1988; White, 1986; White et al., n.d.) suggest they should be presented before any questions are asked that might indicate possible sexual abuse. This is useful if they are to be used as an anatomical model. Boat and Everson (1988) also suggest observing the child in free play with the dolls after they have been presented and before questions are asked. This strategy would allow for the doll use as a diagnostic screen and a memory stimulus.

Others suggest the dolls might be presented later, after the child has begun to disclose or has made a verbal statement (*APSAC Guidelines*, 1995; Faller, 1993). In such cases, the dolls could serve as a demonstration aid, that is, as a means of facilitating descriptive information from a child whose language skills are limited or who is reluctant to talk; as a medium for clarifying verbal statements; or as a way of corroborating disclosures. However, requiring a verbal disclosure first would defeat the use of the dolls as a demonstration aid for children who are fearful or reluctant to disclose, or as a memory stimulus.

Guidelines also vary as to how many dolls the evaluator should present to the child. When describing using the dolls as an anatomical model, authors recommend two, three, or four. As an icebreaker, it might be useful to present four or more so that the child becomes desensitized to the dolls and sees that the evaluator is comfortable talking about private parts, before any questions are asked about possible abuse. However, if the dolls are to be used as a demonstration aid or a memory stimulus, it might be best to assist the child in choosing dolls of the same number, race, age, and gender as the people in the circumstance in which the child may have been sexually abused.

The guidelines that advise use of the dolls as an anatomical model instruct the evaluator to assist the child in undressing them and to have the child identify the body parts and their functions, including the sexual ones. This is good practice because it assures accurate communication about the private parts. In addition, it allows the interviewer to assess some aspects of compe-tency (the child has names for the body parts and knows their functions), and it can serve as a diagnostic screen (the child, in describing the functions of the private parts, reveals advanced sexual knowledge). However, failure to present the dolls in this manner, or only asking the child to identify the private parts because the interviewer is using the dolls as a demonstration aid or a memory stimulus, does not invalidate the assessment.

White advocates only the use of dolls (White, 1986; White, n.d.; White et al., 1986) as an anatomical model and provide 14 questions about body parts, with instructions that the evaluator should ask these about sexual and nonsexual parts. Their advice does not allow for other doll functions. Nor does it allow the evaluator to vary the use of the dolls according to the circumstances of the case.

Faller (1993) has suggested three possible scenarios for doll use, which allow them to serve a variety of functions, and states that these scenarios should not be considered inclusive. The scenarios are as follows. The child may spontaneously initiate interaction with the dolls because they are present in the playroom, and the interviewer facilitates their use. The evaluator introduces the dolls after the child has begun discussion of sexual abuse to facilitate, clarify, or corroborate disclosures. And the interviewer presents the dolls without any cues from the child in order to initiate a discussion of body parts if other attempts to understand whether the child has been sexually abused have been unsuccessful.

Morgan (1995) recommends caution in using anatomical dolls because they have been subject to legal challenges and suggests introducing them after the child has indicated sexual abuse has occurred. She says they may be presented either clothed or unclothed, but clothing may need to be put on for the child to use them to demonstrate the abuse. She recommends a period of unstructured exploration of the dolls after they have been introduced and then a body parts inventory. The interviewer returns to a discussion of the child's prior disclosure after the inventory and asks the child to choose appropriate dolls and demonstrate what happened. Follow-up questions are employed.

To summarize, there are many opinions about how to use the dolls, but none has been empirically demonstrated to be superior or correct. Evaluators are probably safe in taking their cues from the child and varying their doll technique according to the function the dolls are serving and the circumstances of the case. However, the dolls should not be used in a leading manner, for example, asking the child to show with the dolls how or where the alleged perpetrator touched the child when the child has not indicated there was any such activity (*APSAC Guidelines*, 1995; Bruck et al., 1994).

STUDY QUESTIONS

11. How do professionals use the dolls as a diagnostic screen? As a memory stimulus?

12. Discuss the spectrum of opinion regarding the timing of the presentation of the dolls, the number of dolls to be presented, and the manner in which the dolls are introduced.

13. What three scenarios has Faller suggested for doll use?

14. What general guidelines should be followed?

Basic Reference: Anatomical Drawings

Groth, N., & Stevenson, T. (1990). *Anatomical drawings for use in the investigation and intervention of child sexual abuse.* **Dunedin, FL: Forensic Mental Health Associates.**

Groth, a pioneer in work with sex offenders, has collaborated with Stevenson, a medical illustrator, to produce a book of anatomical drawings for use in diagnosis and treatment of sexual abuse, with brief instructions.

Review and Critique

Much less has been written about the use of anatomical drawings in interviewing children thought to have been sexually abused than about anatomical dolls. However, Conte and colleagues (1991) report that almost two thirds of the experts responding to their survey use anatomical drawings, and Kendall-Tackett (1992), in a report from a survey of 201 Boston area professionals assessing sexual abuse, found that 47% employ anatomical drawings.

So far, only one study has examined the utility of anatomical drawings. Steward (1989), as already noted, compared the relative effect of anatomical drawings, verbal questions, anatomical dolls, and a computer-assisted interview on children's ability to recount medical procedures. The anatomical drawings were found to be superior to verbal questioning, although not superior to other media.

Although many medical charts have anatomical drawings, the only ones found for use by nonmedical personnel are those developed by Forensic Mental Health Associates (Groth & Stevenson, 1990). These drawings consist of unclothed front and back views of males and females, white and black, at five different developmental stages—preschool, elementary school, adolescent, adult, and elder. Groth (Groth & Stevenson, 1990), in his directions for the use of the drawings, suggests that the child be given a set of the drawings copied from the booklet and asked to choose the drawing that looks most like her or him and one that looks like the offender. The child is then asked to mark on the drawings where the offender has touched/abused the child, or the child is asked multiple-choice questions about the body parts ("Did he touch you on the penis, the buttocks, or somewhere else?"—pointing to the parts on the drawing). If the child indicates she or he or the offender was clothed or partially clothed, clothing is to be drawn on the pictures. Groth also suggests the drawings might be used to clarify something in a free drawing or as a prelude to the introduction of the anatomical dolls.

Anatomical drawings can serve many of the functions Boat and Everson describe for anatomical dolls. They can be used as an icebreaker, an anatomical model, a demonstration aid, a memory stimulus, and a diagnostic screen. Steward noted that they were less useful than anatomical dolls when children needed to show genital and anal touch, especially penetration. Similarly, Faller (1993) states that it is more difficult for children to demonstrate interaction between two or more individuals with pictures than with the dolls. They may also be of lesser utility as a diagnostic screen or a memory stimulus than the dolls, because they are two dimensional and there is no opportunity to undress them.

However, they have a distinct advantage over the dolls in that the copies employed in the interview can become a part of the case record. The evaluator or child writes on the relevant drawings the names the child gives for body parts, as the drawings are used as an anatomical model. Likewise, remarks the child makes as the drawings are used as a diagnostic screen or a memory stimulus can be written on the drawings. Finally, of course the evaluator can ask the child to indicate on the drawings whom they represent and the location of any sexual touch or activity. If the child can write, the child can be instructed to write on the drawing. If not, the interviewer can record the child's statements on the drawing. It is also a good practice for the evaluator to write any questions she or he asked when using the drawings (Faller, 1993). As part of the case record, the drawings are admissible under the business records exception to the hearsay rule in litigation, and therefore become an exhibit for the factfinder to review when arriving at a decision about abuse.

Perhaps another advantage that anatomical drawings have over anatomical dolls is that they have not been the subject of as much controversy.

STUDY QUESTIONS

15. What has research shown regarding the utility of anatomical drawings?
    a. Describe the various functions of anatomical drawings.
    b. In terms of usefulness, how do they compare to anatomical dolls?
    c. What procedure is suggested by Groth for the use of the drawings?

Picture Drawing

Another medium that can be used to assess children and elicit information from them is picture drawing. Conte and colleagues (1991) found that 87% of respondents from their study used free drawings when evaluating sexual abuse allegations. A smaller number—less than half—of Kendall-Tackett's (1992) Boston area respondents used drawings.

Review and Critique

Although the APSAC guidelines for evaluation of sexual abuse (1990) mention drawings as one means of eliciting information about possible sexual abuse, they do not elaborate. In contrast, the AACAP guidelines (1990) have a separate section on the use of children's drawings, with suggestions for drawing tasks and some guidelines regarding interpreting drawings.

RESEARCH ON FREE DRAWINGS

Some research has been undertaken that attempts to differentiate characteristics of free drawings of sexually abused children from nonabused children. Several studies have focused on the sexual body parts in free drawings. Yates, Beutler, and Crago (1985), using free drawings with 18 sexually abused girls and 17 disturbed nonabused girls ranging from ages 3½ to 17, found that the sexually abused children were likely either to exaggerate and focus on the sexual parts of the body or to avoid them. In one study, Hibbard, Roghmann, and Hoekelman (1987) found that 57 of the 3- to 7-year-old children assessed for sexual abuse were six to eight times (the variation based on whether they were suspected or confirmed cases) more likely to draw genitalia than were 55 nonabused children. However, the rates of genital drawings were quite low for both groups. In a later study by Hibbard and Hartmann (1990) with 65 victims and 64 nonvictims, only victims drew genitalia in their pictures, but the number was so small that differences were not statistically significant. Friedrich (1990) provides comparative data from parental responses to the Child Sexual Behavior Inventory. Parents of children referred for sexual abuse are more likely to report that their children include genitals in their drawings than children not referred for sexual abuse. However, Friedrich notes that some nonreferred children also were reported to have drawn genitalia. These findings suggest that in the few instances when children draw genitals, this is cause for concern and further inquiry. However, it would be inappropriate to make a diagnosis of sexual abuse based on the presence (or absence) of sexual parts in a child's drawing.

Another approach to the use of drawings is that developed by Burgess and colleagues (e.g., Burgess & Hartman, 1993; Burgess, McCausland, & Wolbert, 1981). They instruct evaluators to have children draw seven separate pictures: (a) your favorite weather, (b) your whole self as a younger child, (c) your whole self today, (d) the family doing something together (the Kinetic Family Drawing), (e) what happened to you (i.e., the sexual abuse), (f) a house and a tree, and (g) your own drawing (free drawing).

Burgess and Hartman (1993) describe each of these drawings and drawing tasks as having a specific function in the assessment process. They state that such drawings should be used as an "associative tool for memory" and caution that those interpreting drawings should be professionals trained in interpreting artwork.

Several studies have used this series of drawings. Burgess, Hartman, Wolbert, and Grant (1987) had 81 drawings of sexually abused children who testified in court rated by six clinicians skilled in the use of drawings with sexually abused children. They found indicators of numerous psychosocial sequelae of sexual abuse in the children's drawings, for example, anxiety, insecurity, isolation, body image problems, regression, and repeated memories of the abuse.

Elizabeth Burgess (1988) also employed this schema in research with a sample of nine children sexually abused in day care and eight comparison children. She examined 53 characteristics of these two sets of drawings and noted differences in percentages of such traits in the two groups. However, no statistical analyses were presented. Nevertheless, she found that the drawings of sexually abused children depicted an avoidance of drawing the sexual abuse, omission and sexualization of body parts, sad and affectless mood, and anxiety. She also found evidence of the success of therapy in the abused children.

Finally, Burgess and colleagues (Howe, Burgess, & McCormack, 1987) had 124 runaway adolescents, 53 of whom reported sexual abuse, engage in this drawing exercise. Statistically significant differences were found in psychiatric diagnoses based on the drawings, specifically, psychotic, avoidant, anxious-avoidant, and anxious-aggressive. Because this drawing exercise has been interpreted in a variety of ways, its generalizability is limited.

There have been other attempts to examine the affective content of drawings of children who may have been sexually abused. Chantler and colleagues (1993), in a study cited earlier that also involved the use of the

Louisville Behavior Checklist, asked participants to "draw a whole person." Participants were sexually abused, clinic, and community samples. Their pictures were then scored according to Koppitz's 30 Emotional Indicators and six flag items for maladjustment. Although there were significant differences in findings on both measures by group, predictive validity was quite modest. The authors suggest caution in using this drawing task to decide whether children have been sexually abused.

A somewhat different approach is taken by Kaufman and Wohl (1992) in a book on drawings of sexually abused children. They scored the House-Tree-Person and Kinetic Family Drawings on 86 items that they decided were indicative of Finkelhor's (1986) four categories of traumatagenic impact from sexual abuse: betrayal (24 items), traumatic sexualization (32 items), stigmatization (19 items), and powerlessness (11 items). Only a small number of these 86 items are noted. Children from high-certainty sexual abuse cases were compared to clinic and community samples, with 18 children ages 5 to 10 in each group. There are some statistically significant differences among groups on total scores, but none on the items within the categories of betrayal and powerlessness and only one each on sexualization and stigmatization. Moreover, although no statistic is provided, the clinic sample is over a year older than the other two groups, and no post hoc tests to look at between-groups differences were conducted after the ANOVAs. Thus, the approach developed by Kaufman and Wohl is interesting and may well have merit but cannot be evaluated as it is presented.

CLINICAL USES OF FREE DRAWINGS

From a clinical perspective, a number of authors have offered suggestions regarding specific drawing tasks that might elicit information relevant to sexual abuse. Children may first be asked to draw anything, and their choice of subject may be revealing (Faller, 1988). They may be asked to draw themselves (Benedek & Schetky, 1987; Faller, 1988; Friedrich, 1990) and then tell something about the picture, such as what makes them happy, sad, angry, and scared (Faller, 1993). They might also be asked to draw their family or the Kinetic Family Drawing, that is, their family doing something (AACAP, 1990; Benedek & Schetky, 1987; Faller, 1993; Friedrich, 1990). Any of these drawing exercises may yield information helpful in assessment for possible sexual abuse.

Another potentially useful drawing task is one described by Hewitt and Arrowood (1994), called the Touch Continuum. It actually is two drawing tasks, and most of the drawing is done by the interviewer. Hewitt and

Arrowood recommend this strategy for children ages 4 to 8 and note findings on 42 children, whose drawing outputs are compared to clinical conclusions about sexual abuse. The first task involves dividing a piece of paper into four boxes and drawing faces in each to represent happy, sad, mad, and scared affects. The interviewer then encourages the child to label the emotion in each face. The second task begins with the interviewer dividing a piece of paper into six boxes. Stick figures that represent the child are drawn in each box, and the interviewer labels or has the child label the box hugging, tickling, spanking, kissing, hitting, and private-parts touching. Each type of touch is discussed with the child in terms of the feelings it generates, the body parts involved, and the persons who touch the child in that way. This drawing task may elicit information about physical and sexual abuse. The authors present findings comparing Touch Continuum data to conclusions based on a comprehensive assessment of possible sexual abuse. There were no false positives from the Touch Continuum data, but a high rate of false negatives.

Drawings that are likely to be more to the point and less open to a variety of interpretations are the following: a picture of the alleged offender, the place where the sexual abuse occurred, an instrument that might have been used in the abuse, or the abusive act itself (Benedek & Schetky, 1987; Faller, 1993; Friedrich, 1990). Although Benedek and Schetky emphasize the importance of the affect in the picture, having the child write or writing for the child who and what in pictures that is relevant to the sexual abuse can render it a piece of evidence that is clinically and legally convincing and admissible in court as a part of the business record (Faller, 1993). Charles Wilson (personal communication, 1992) favors a focus on drawings that depict aspects of the abuse rather than more general pictures that may contain themes the evaluator interprets.

STUDY QUESTIONS

16. What has research shown regarding the different characteristics of drawings by sexually abused children and non-sexually abused children?

    a. What approach is suggested by Burgess and colleagues for the use of drawings in assessment?

    b. What suggestions have other authors offered regarding specific drawing tasks that may elicit information relevant to sexual abuse?

17. How can the risk of evaluator misinterpretation be decreased?

References

American Academy of Child and Adolescent Psychiatry (AACAP). *Guidelines for the evaluation of child and adolescent sexual abuse.* (Modified December 14, 1990). (Available from AACAP, 3615 Wisconsin Ave. N.W., Washington, DC 20016)

American Professional Society on the Abuse of Children. (1995). *Guidelines for use of anatomical dolls during investigative interviews of children who may have been sexually abused.* [Available from the American Professional Society on the Abuse of Children, 407 S. Dearborn, Suite 1300, Chicago, IL 60605.]

American Professional Society on the Abuse of Children. (n. d.). *Guidelines for psychosocial evaluation of suspected sexual abuse in young children.* [Available from the American Professional Society on the Abuse of Children, 407 S. Dearborn, Suite 1300, Chicago, IL 60605.]

August, R., & Foreman, B. (1989). A comparison of sexually abused and non-sexually abused children's behavioral responses to anatomically correct dolls. *Child Psychiatry and Human Development, 20*(1), 39-47.

Bays, J. (1990). Are the genitalia of anatomical dolls distorted? *Child Abuse & Neglect, 14,* 171-175.

Benedek, E., & Schetky, D. (1987). Problems in validating allegations of sexual abuse: Part 2. Clinical evaluation. *Journal of the American Academy of Child and Adolescent Psychiatry, 26,* 916-921.

Boat, B., & Everson, M. (1988). Interviewing young children with anatomical dolls. *Child Welfare, 67,* 337-352.

Boat, B., & Everson, M. (1994). Exploration of anatomical dolls by non-referred preschool-aged children. *Child Abuse & Neglect, 18*(2), 139-154.

Britton, H., & O'Keefe, M. A. (1991). Use of nonanatomical dolls in the sexual abuse interview. *Child Abuse & Neglect, 15,* 567-573.

Bruck, M., Ceci, S., Francoueur, E., & Renick, A. (1995). Anatomically detailed dolls do not facilitate preschoolers' reports of a pediatric examination involving genital touching. *Journal of Experimental Psychology: Applied (1)2,* 95-109.

Burgess, A., & Hartman, C. (1993). Children's drawings. *Child Abuse & Neglect, 17,* 161-168.

Burgess, A., Hartman, C., Wolbert, W., & Grant, C. (1987). Child molestation: Assessing impact in multiple victims. *Archives of Psychiatric Nursing, 1*(1), 33-39.

Burgess, A., McCausland, M., & Wolbert, W. (1981). Children's drawings as indicators of sexual trauma. *Perspectives in Psychiatric Care, 14,* 50-58.

Burgess, E. (1988). Sexually abused children and their drawings. *Archives of Psychiatric Nursing, 2*(2), 65-73.

Chantler, L., Pelco, L., & Mertin, P. (1993). The psychological evaluation of child sexual abuse using the Louisville Behavior Checklist and Human Figure Drawing. *Child Abuse & Neglect, 17,* 271-280.

Cohn, D. (1991). Anatomical doll play of preschoolers referred for sexual abuse and those not referred. *Child Abuse & Neglect, 15,* 455-466.

Conte, J., Sorenson, E., Fogarty, L., & Dalla Rosa, J. (1991). Evaluating children's reports of sexual abuse: Results from a survey of professionals. *American Journal of Orthopsychiatry, 61,* 428-437.

Dawson, B., Vaughan, A., & Wagner, W. (1992). Normal responses to sexually anatomically detailed dolls. *Journal of Family Violence, 7,* 135-152.

Everson, M., & Boat, B. (1990). Sexualized doll play among young children: Implications for the use of anatomical dolls in sexual abuse evaluations. *Journal of the American Academy of Child and Adolescent Psychiatry, 29,* 736-742.

Everson, M., & Boat, B. (1994). Putting the anatomical doll controversy in perspective: An examination of the major uses and criticisms of the dolls in child sexual abuse evaluations. *Child Abuse & Neglect, 18,* 113-130.

Faller, K. C. (1988). *Child sexual abuse: An interdisciplinary manual for diagnosis, case management, and treatment.* New York: Columbia University Press.

Faller, K. C. (1993). *Child sexual abuse: Assessment and intervention issues.* Washington, DC: U.S. Department of Health and Human Services, National Center on Child Abuse & Neglect.

Finkelhor, D. (1986). *Sourcebook on child sexual abuse.* Beverly Hills, CA: Sage.

Friedrich, W. (1990). *Psychotherapy of sexually abused children and their families.* New York: Norton.

Goodman, G., & Aman, C. (1990). Children's use of anatomically correct dolls to recount an event. *Child Development, 61,* 1859-1871.

Groth, N., & Stevenson, T. (1990). *Anatomical drawings for use in the investigation and intervention of child sexual abuse.* Dunedin, FL: Forensic Mental Health Associates.

Hewitt, S., & Arrowood, A. (1994). Systematic touch exploration as a screening procedure for child abuse: A pilot study. *Journal of Child Sexual Abuse, 3*(2), 31-43.

Hibbard, R. A., & Hartmann, G. (1990). Emotional indicators in human figure drawings of sexually victimized and nonabused children. *Journal of Clinical Psychology, 46,* 211-219.

Hibbard, R. A., Roghmann, K., & Hoekelman, R. A. (1987). Genitalia in children's drawings: An association with sexual abuse. *Pediatrics, 79,* 129-137.

Howe, J., Burgess, A., & McCormack, A. (1987). Adolescent runaways and their drawings. *Arts and Psychotherapy, 14,* 35-40.

Jampole, L., & Webber, M. (1987). An assessment of the behavior of sexually abused and non-sexually abused children with anatomically correct dolls. *Child Abuse & Neglect, 11,* 187-192.

Kaufman, B., & Wohl, A. (1992). *Casualties of childhood: A developmental perspective on sexual abuse using projective drawings.* New York: Brunner/Mazel.

Kendall-Tackett, K. (1992). Beyond anatomical dolls: Professionals' use of other play therapy techniques. *Child Abuse & Neglect, 16,* 139-142.

Kendall-Tackett, K., & Watson, M. (1991). Factors that influence professionals' perceptions of behavioral indicators of child sexual abuse. *Journal of Interpersonal Violence, 6,* 385-395.

Leventhal, J., Hamilton, J., Rekedal, S., Tebano-Micci, A., & Eyster, C. (1989). Anatomically correct dolls used in interviews of young children suspected of having been sexually abused. *Pediatrics, 84,* 900-906.

Maan, C. (1991). Assessment of sexually abused children with anatomically detailed dolls: A critical review. *Behavioral Sciences and the Law, 9,* 43-51.

Morgan, M., with Edwards, V. (1995). *How to interview sexual abuse victims: Including the use of anatomical dolls.* Thousand Oaks, CA: Sage.

Ney, T., (Ed.). (1995). *True and false allegations of child sexual abuse.* New York: Brunner/Mazel.

Robin, M. (1991). *Assessing child maltreatment reports: The problem of false allegations.* New York: Haworth.

Sivan, A., Schor, D., Koeppl, G., & Noble, L. (1988). Interaction of normal children with anatomical dolls. *Child Abuse & Neglect, 12,* 295-304.

Steward, M. (1989, November). *The development of a model interview for young child victims of sexual abuse* (Final report to National Center on Child Abuse and Neglect). Davis: University of California, Davis, Department of Psychiatry.

White, S. (1986). Uses and abuses of the sexually anatomically correct dolls. *APA Division of Child, Youth, and Family Services Newsletter, 9*(1), 3-4.

White, S., Strom, G., Santilli, G., & Halpin, B. (1986). Interviewing young sexual abuse victims with anatomically correct dolls. *Child Abuse & Neglect, 10,* 519-529.

White, S., Strom, G., Santilli, G., & Quinn, K. (n.d.). *Guidelines for interviewing preschoolers with sexually anatomically detailed dolls.* Cleveland, OH: Case Western Reserve University School of Medicine.

Yates, A., Beutler, L., & Crago, M. (1985). Drawings by child victims of abuse. *Child Abuse & Neglect, 9,* 183-189.

Special Considerations for Cases Involving Very Young Children

Basic Reference

Hewitt, S., and Friedrich, W. (1995). Assessment and management of abuse allegations with very young children. In T. Ney, (Ed.), *True and false allegations of child sexual abuse* (pp. 125-139). New York: Brunner/Mazel.

This article presents the current thought on characteristics of sexually abused children under age 3 and how to assess them.

Review and Critique

Both clinicians and researchers often note that "very young children" present particular challenges in terms of assessment for possible sexual abuse, often

60

without specifying the ages of these children. Designating children 3 years and under as very young children is a good practical definition; however, as pointed out by Goodman (1992), developmental age is more important than chronological age. Hewitt and Friedrich (1991a, 1991b, 1995; Hewitt, 1993), Haynes-Seman (1991), James (1989), and Everson (1992) have been particularly interested in the evaluation of very young children.

It is safe to say that the police officer or child protection investigator will not have the time, and in many instances the skills, to adequately assess children 3 years and younger. Nevertheless, in such cases, the physical evidence from the "crime scene," which can be collected only by law enforcement, may be especially crucial to understanding what may or may not have happened to the very young child. More information is provided about police evidence later in the study guide.

Little research has been conducted on evaluation of very young children. However, Hewitt and Friedrich have examined their respective clinical samples of preschoolers, including those age 3 and under, from both research and clinical perspectives. In one study (Hewitt & Friedrich, 1991a), they found significant differences in scores of 43 children age 3 and under who had probably been sexually abused and those who had probably not been sexually abused on the Child Sexual Behavior Inventory and sleep problems as rated on the Achenbach Child Sexual Behavior Inventory (Achenbach, Edelbrock, & Howell, 1987). Similarly, Hewitt (1993) reported on 21 children age 2 and attempts to differentiate between those who were sexually abused and those who were not. She noted that all of those determined to have been sexually abused had elevated levels of sexualized play and sleep disturbance.

Most approaches to evaluating young children place considerable reliance on information provided by the child's caretaker (Everson, 1992; Hewitt & Friedrich, 1991a, 1991b, 1995). In the case of Hewitt and Friedrich, this includes information from the Child Behavior Checklist, which has a version for 2- and 3-year-olds (Achenbach et al., 1987), and the Sexual Behavior Inventory (Friedrich, 1990), which is validated for children beginning at age 2. In addition, a careful history is taken from the caretaker about the child. Particular emphasis is placed on any observation of sexualized behavior, statements indicating sexual knowledge, and statements that might indicate sexual abuse. Trigger events (e.g., bathtime, bedtime) and the place of these indicators in the larger context of the child's life are ascertained. In addition, associated behavior problems, such as sleep disturbance, tantrums, diapering refusal, fears, and skill regression are carefully documented (Everson, 1992; Hewitt, 1993; Hewitt & Friedrich, 1995).

In contrast to an approach that encourages reliance on information from the (nonaccused) caretaker is that advocated by Haynes-Seman (Haynes-Seman & Baumgarten, 1994; Haynes-Seman & Hart, 1988; Haynes-Seman & Krugman, 1989). She is skeptical of such information because of potential caretaker bias (Haynes-Seman & Baumgarten, 1994) and believes that observing the interaction between the alleged abuser and the child can be the key to determining whether a young child, with limited verbal skills, has been sexually abused. Hewitt and Friedrich (1991b) have challenged this contention, stating that "given the relative lack of autonomy in children of this age, face-to-face interaction of the child with a perpetrator may impair the evaluation process" (p. 3). Similarly, as noted earlier, Faller et al. (1991) have rejected the use of parent-child interaction as a viable method of assessing the likelihood of sexual abuse.

S T U D Y   Q U E S T I O N S

1. What strategies have been suggested for evaluating children age 3 and under?

2. What weight is given to information provided by the child's caretaker?

3. What types of behavior problems should be documented?

Generally, authors on the subject of evaluations of very young children suggest the use of several interviews. Hewitt and Friedrich (1991b) report an average of 3 to 6 hours of child contact and two to four appointments. Everson (1992) says these children require six or more sessions of short duration before an opinion can be formed.

The interviewer is alert to themes in the child's play, with self, and in statements, for example, when using the sand tray or the dollhouse, or with items resembling the alleged abuse situation (Everson, 1992) that suggest possible sexual abuse or fears related to abuse. From time to time, the evaluator constructs scenarios using a variety of media that may elicit themes that could enlighten the evaluator about possible sexual abuse. Often children of this age find it easier to demonstrate sexual acts on their own bodies, rather than with anatomical dolls (Everson, 1992).

Children's memory precedes the time when they can verbally communicate it (Hewitt, 1993). Because of this, clinicians assessing young children often extend their evaluations until children can adequately speak about what they recall. In a recent report, Hewitt (1994) describes two cases of children who were traumatically sexually victimized when they were preverbal but who later gave verbal accounts. One child was 2 years 7 months when abused and 4 when she reported it. The other was 2 years 1 month when victimized and 6 when she disclosed.

STUDY QUESTIONS

4. What types of themes should be noted in the child's play?
5. How many sessions are recommended prior to the formation of an opinion?
6. Why do clinicians often extend their evaluations of very young children?

References

Achenbach, T., Edelbrock, C., & Howell, C. (1987). Empirically-based assessment of behavioral/emotional problems of 2- to 3-year-old children. *Journal of Abnormal Child Psychology, 15*, 629-650.

Everson, M. (1992, January). *Models of sexual abuse evaluations.* Presentation given at the Conference on the Health Science Response to Child Maltreatment, San Diego, CA. (Summary available from Mark Everson, Program on Childhood Abuse and Trauma, Department of Psychiatry, CB 7160, University of North Carolina, Chapel Hill, NC 27599-7160)

Faller, K. C., Froning, M., & Lipovsky, J. (1991). The parent-child interview: Use in evaluating child allegations of sexual abuse by a parent. *American Journal of Orthopsychiatry, 61*, 552-557.

Friedrich, W. (1990). *Psychotherapy of sexually abused children and their families.* New York: Norton.

Goodman, G. (1992, October). *Children's eyewitness testimony.* Paper presented at the Midwest Conference on Child Sexual Abuse, Madison, WI.

Haynes-Seman, C. (1991, October). *Assessment of allegations of sexual abuse in divorce.* Paper presented at the National Conference on Child Abuse and Neglect, Denver.

Haynes-Seman, C., & Baumgarten, D. (1994). *Children speak for themselves.* New York: Bruner/Mazel.

Haynes-Seman, C., & Hart, J. S. (1988). Interactional assessment: Evaluation of parent-child relationships in abuse and neglect. In D. Bross, R. Krugman, M. Lenherr, D. A. Rosenberg, & B. Schmitt (Eds.), *The new child protection team handbook* (pp. 181-198). New York: Garland.

Haynes-Seman, C., & Krugman, R. (1989). Sexualized attention: Normal interaction or precursor to sexual abuse? *American Journal of Orthopsychiatry, 59,* 391-400.

Hewitt, S. (1993, January). *Assessment of very young children.* Paper presented at the Conference on the Health Science Response to Child Maltreatment, San Diego, CA.

Hewitt, S. (1994). Preverbal sexual abuse: What two children report in later years. *Child Abuse and Neglect, 18,* 821-826.

Hewitt, S., & Friedrich, W. (1991a). Effects of probable sexual abuse on preschool children. In M. Q. Patton (Ed.), *Family sexual abuse.* Newbury Park, CA: Sage.

Hewitt, S., & Friedrich, W. (1991b). *Assessing sexual abuse in very young children.* Unpublished manuscript. (Available from S. Hewitt, 3300 Edinborough Way, Suite 418, Edina, MN 55435)

Hewitt, S., & Friedrich, W. (1995). Assessment and management of abuse allegations with very young children. In T. Ney (Ed.), *True and false allegations of sexual child sexual abuse* (pp. 125-139). New York: Brunner/Mazel.

James, B. (1989). *Treating traumatized children.* Lexington, MA: Lexington Books.

9

Children as Witnesses

Basic References

Doris, J. (Ed.). (1991). *The suggestibility of children's recollections.* **Washington, DC: American Psychological Association.**

This volume represents the current state of knowledge and debate regarding children as witnesses. It consists of summaries by researchers of their studies and findings and commentaries by other researchers.

Perry, N., & Wrightsman, L. (1991). *The child witness.* **Newbury Park, CA: Sage.**

This book summarizes information about children in court; reactions to child witnesses; child development; children's ability to understand, remember, and communicate; and the dilemma of trying to protect the rights of all parties in legal proceedings. It proposes some remedies to problems of child witnesses.

Review and Critique

Unlike other types of child maltreatment, sexual abuse usually does not produce physical findings (found only in 10% to 35% of cases). Generally, the most important evidence is the child's statement (and in some cases, behavior). In part, because of the centrality of the child's role, there has been a great deal of interest in and concern about the accuracy of children's statements regarding their sexual abuse. This issue has been the focus of clinical observations, professional opinion, and research. The research will be discussed in this section.

CHARACTERISTICS OF THE RESEARCH

The body of research is substantial. Because ethically it would be unacceptable to expose children to sexual abuse and then assess the accuracy of their accounts of these experiences, the research consists of analogue studies. In these studies, researchers construct an experience (e.g., a child goes into a trailer with a stranger and engages in certain activities; Goodman, Rudy, Bottoms, & Aman, 1990) or take advantage of a naturally occurring event in the child's life (e.g., a medical exam; Bruck et al., 1994; Saywitz, Goodman, Nicholas, & Moan, 1989; Steward, 1989). These experiences are documented, either on videotape or with written notes, so that the child's account can be judged against what actually took place. The child is then questioned after the experience, sometimes with the use of leading, trick, or coercive questions.

In some studies, attempts are made to contaminate children's recall by providing them with misleading information, either before, during, or after being exposed to the experience (Leichtman & Ceci, 1995; Lindberg, 1991; Loftus & Davies, 1984; Peters, 1991; Zaragoza, 1991). The accuracy of children at different developmental stages has been addressed (Goodman & Aman, 1990; Gordon et al., 1993). In addition, researchers have examined the effect of a supportive versus an unsupportive interviewer (Goodman & Clarke-Stewart, 1991) and the impact of a delay between the event and the questioning (Goodman, Wilson, Hazan, & Reed, 1991). Researchers have also experimented with methods for enhancing children's ability to recall experiences (Goodman & Clarke-Stewart, 1991; Saywitz, Nathanson, Snyder, & Lamphear, 1993). Finally, some studies (cited in earlier chapters of the study guide) compare different methods for eliciting information from children (e.g., questioning with anatomical dolls vs. questioning without props).

THE ISSUE OF ECOLOGICAL VALIDITY

An important factor to assess in determining the relevance of this research to children reporting sexual abuse is its ecological validity. There are two aspects to this. The first is the extent to which the events the child is exposed to are comparable to experiences of sexual abuse. The second is the degree to which the questioning techniques and other strategies employed by the researchers are similar to methods that clinicians and others investigating sexual abuse use.

With regard to the ecological validity of the events, situations in which the child actually participates, rather than views a movie or slides, are more relevant. Research that involves acts that might be like sexual abuse, for example, genital and anal touching in a medical exam (Bruck et al., 1995; Saywitz et al., 1989; Steward, 1989), dressing and undressing (Bruck et al., 1994; Goodman & Aman, 1987, 1990), picture taking (Goodman & Aman, 1987, 1990), and high levels of stress (Peters, 1991; Steward, 1989) are useful. Similarly, research in which children are admonished not to tell about the event (Goodman & Clarke-Stewart, 1991) or are required to identify a "perpetrator" resemble situations of sexual abuse (Goodman & Clarke-Stewart, 1991; Peters, 1991). However, as Robin (1991, p. 99) points out, researchers cannot re-create events with the profound effects and the "web of involvements" characteristic of the crime of sexual abuse.

As to the ecological validity of questioning procedures, those that employ props such as anatomical dolls are obviously germane. The research that explores the relative merits of free recall versus yes-no questions is also important. Finally, studies that look at the effect of leading or suggestive questions, manipulations of children's reactions, and attempts at programming should be considered. Perhaps less relevant are situations where researchers ask misleading questions, such as what color scarf the nurse was wearing when the nurse was not wearing a scarf, and studies where there are deliberate and elaborate attempts to contaminate the child's recollection.

S T U D Y   Q U E S T I O N S

1. How has research on children as witnesses been conceptualized?

   a. Why is ecological validity an important factor to assess in determining the relevance of this research?

   b. Which research conditions seem most relevant to the investigation of child sexual assault? Least relevant?

The discussion of this research will be divided into findings regarding children's memory and children's suggestibility.

Children's Memory

Neither adults nor children record experiences in their minds with 100% accuracy. Nevertheless, children do remember past events, and older (age 10 and above) children have memories that are as good as those of adults (Perry & Wrightsman, 1991).

One of the reasons for superior memories of older children is they have a context of life experiences that is used to interpret and encode events (Brainerd & Ornstein, 1991). Children's recall is better for experiences in which they actively participate (Goodman & Aman, 1990). In one study (Goodman et al., 1989) in which there was a significant delay (of about 4 years) between the experience and the questioning, few children spontaneously recalled the event, and focused questions were necessary. However, the event they were being asked to remember, activities with a male researcher, might be less memorable than sexual abuse.

Young children have better recall of salient events in their life (Brainerd & Ornstein, 1991) such as a school trip, and of central aspects of the experience than of peripheral ones (Goodman & Clarke-Stewart, 1991). They also have good recollection of repeated events in their lives (Brainerd & Ornstein, 1991).

Young children (3- and 4-year-olds) have particular difficulty with spontaneous recall and usually require specific questions to trigger their memories. Gordon and colleagues (1993) questioned 3- and 5-year-olds about a medical exam that occurred 3 weeks earlier. When asked to tell what happened at their check-ups, 3-year-olds reported less than one fifth of what occurred, but they recalled close to 70% when direct questions were added. The 5-year-olds did better, but the differences were not statistically significant.

Children also appear less likely to spontaneously report certain types of information than others. In a study by Saywitz, Goodman, and colleagues (Saywitz et al., 1989), 36 girls ages 5 and 7 received a genital and anal exam as part of a general physical examination, and 36 received a scoliosis exam. The vast majority of those receiving the genital (78%) and anal (89%) exam did not mention it when asked to describe the physical, but all children who received the scoliosis exam reported it. The researchers concluded that children were unwilling to describe private-parts experiences to an interviewer. This finding suggests the necessity of asking direct questions when querying about possible sexual abuse. Indeed, when the researchers did this, the proportion of children accurately reporting receiving a genital exam increased to 86% and an anal exam to 69%, and there were only three false positives.

However, direct questions may not be useful with 3-year-olds (Bruck et al., 1995). In a similar study, but without a free-recall condition, half or fewer boys and girls who received genital and anal exams reported these in response to direct questions. As noted in the section on anatomical dolls in Chapter 7, a possible explanation for the findings may lie in the nature of the exam. It consisted of a light touch on the genitals and buttocks. Arguably, these events were less memorable than many situations employed in analogue studies. This study also generated an unusually high percentage of false positives, which will be discussed in the next section under children's suggestibility.

Children under age 10 have difficulty remembering persons seen briefly or identifying them when in disguise (Perry & Wrightsman, 1991). They also have trouble picking out perpetrators from a photo line-up, but do better with a live line-up (Perry & Wrightsman, 1991), as long as their (children's) identities are protected. Even in situations where the perpetrator is a stranger, children fail to implicate him when asked about him in his presence (Peters, 1991). Moreover, when they have been admonished by the perpetrator not to tell, a substantial majority will not, even though he is not there (Goodman & Clarke-Stewart, 1991).

The findings regarding the effect of stress on memory are mixed, with some researchers finding that stress decreases the accuracy of recall (Peters, 1991) and others not finding this decrease (Goodman & Clarke-Stewart, 1991).

Researchers have examined strategies that might enhance children's recall. For example, Saywitz and colleagues (1993) trained 6- to 11-year-olds to use generic cue cards to remind them to report five forensically relevant categories of information: participants (who), setting (where), actions (what), conversations/affective states, and resolution. This technique, called narrative elaboration, was demonstrated to significantly improve spontaneous recall without an increase in errors.

STUDY QUESTIONS

2. What is generally known about the characteristics of children's memory?
3. What types of information do children seem less likely to spontaneously report?
4. How do children most often respond when asked to identify a "perpetrator"?

In their study, Saywitz and colleagues (1993) also report experiments that teach children strategies to enhance accurate communication with an interviewer, inoculate children against the stress of the courtroom setting, and improve their resistance to misleading questions. The last study will be described in the next section.

Children's Suggestibility

OMISSION VERSUS COMMISSION ERRORS

Children are fairly resistant to suggestive (or leading, according to Faller's typology) questions (Goodman et al., 1990), although younger children (3- and 4-year-olds) are more suggestible than older ones. In most studies, children are more likely to make errors of omission than errors of commission (Goodman & Aman, 1990; Goodman & Clarke-Stewart, 1991; Saywitz, Goodman, & Myers, 1990), that is, more likely to say no when the correct response is yes than to say yes when the correct response is no to a yes-no question. For instance, in the study by Saywitz, Goodman, and colleagues (1989) involving medical exams, even when a yes-no question was employed, about 15% of the children still did not disclose the genital and anal exam. As already noted, in contrast only three children in the scoliosis condition gave false positive responses to yes-no questions about vaginal and anal touching. Only one gave a response that was more than a simple yes. One girl, when asked about anal touching, said that the doctor touched her with a stick. These three false positives make up 1% of responses to all questions regarding private-part touching and derive from 8% of the children receiving the scoliosis exam. Only the child stating that the doctor touched her with a stick provided the kind of detail that might lead clinicians to make a positive finding (Mark Everson, personal communication, 1993).

However, Bruck and colleagues' (1995) study, already discussed, which has some similarities to the one just described, has different findings. This study involved considerably younger children, 3-year-olds, and boys as well as girls, half of whom received a private-parts exam as part of a regular physical. The boys who did not receive the genital and anal exam were more resistant than girls to yes-no and misleading questions, demonstrating 75% and 81% accuracy when anatomical dolls were used. The accuracy of the 12 girls, who did not have a private-parts exam, is only about 50% regardless of condition. It is difficult to compare and interpret these findings because the authors do not provide a breakdown that differentiates anal from genital findings.

The 3-year-old girls in the study by Gordon and colleagues (1993) discussed earlier did better than those in Bruck and colleagues' study, but still produced one third false positives. These girls were asked about 20 procedures that are part of a routine medical exam, some of which they had experienced and some they had not. As well, the girls were asked about eight events that are not components of a medical exam. Half might be encountered with another professional, such as a dentist, and half were nonsense, such as "Did the doctor lick your knee?" As already noted, the questioning occurred 3 weeks after the exam. Thus, the task these children were asked to perform was quite difficult. The 5-year-olds in this study did significantly better than the 3-year-olds, answering on average 78% of these misleading questions correctly.

Taken together, findings from the work of Bruck and colleagues (1995) and Gordon and colleagues (1993) argue against reliance on direct questions with very young children as the primary source of information in sexual abuse evaluations and in favor of the sort of extended evaluation that uses data from a range of sources as described earlier in the study guide.

S T U D Y   Q U E S T I O N S

5. In general, how resistant are children to leading questions?

 a. Are children more likely to make errors of commission or omission?

 b. What age group is more likely to give false positive responses?

6. What do findings from the work of Bruck et al. and Gordon et al. suggest regarding reliance on direct questions with very young children?

 How are their findings difficult to interpret?

RESEARCH ON THE USE
OF POSITIVE REINFORCEMENT

Concerns have been raised about the risk of children giving false accounts of sexual abuse because of positive reinforcement by the interviewer (Wakefield & Underwager, 1988). Two studies have addressed that concern (Carter, Bottoms, & Levine, 1995; Goodman, Bottoms, Schwartz-Kennedy, & Rudy, 1991). Goodman and her colleagues, in a study of 72 children ages 3 to 7 who received inoculations, found that the use of positive reinforcement did not affect the accuracy of accounts of the older children, but it did of the younger children. Younger children who received frequent smiles, cookies, and juice gave more accurate and complete accounts of their experiences than did children interviewed by a more distant researcher. In a more recent study with a similiar design, Carter and colleagues (1995) found minimal effects of interviewer style. However, based on existing research, Reed (1993) advises forensic interviewers to be friendly, not authoritarian.

Although leading or suggestive questions, such as "The man touched your private parts, didn't he?" do not appear to result in high numbers of false positive responses except with very young children (Goodman & Clarke-Stewart, 1991), adults can contaminate children's accounts and can program children by using repeated coercive and suggestive questioning. When pieces of misleading information about an experience are communicated to the child, this information can be incorporated into their accounts (Loftus & Davies, 1984; Zaragoza, 1991). The research that supports this finding typically involves changing a detail about a series of slides concerning everyday life, or similar situations, rather than the construction of an entire experience. For example, as the researcher recounts scenes the child has observed, she or he changes the type of stuffed toy that was present, from, say, a dog to a bear. However, it is not clear in those cases where children's accounts are contaminated whether their memories have been altered or whether they are merely telling the interviewer what they think she or he wants to hear (Zaragoza, 1991).

Studies that demonstrate the effects of interrogation have greater ecological validity than the type of study just described. One such study involved interrogation of 5- and 6-year-old children, insisting on a particular interpretation of an ambiguous experience. Most children acquiesced to the interviewer's interpretation. Clarke-Stewart, Thompson, and Lapore (1989) exposed children to a "janitor" who was supposed to be cleaning a playroom. In one condition, the janitor made statements indicating he was really playing with the toys and in the other his comments communicated he was cleaning. The children were then questioned by a researcher who identified herself as the "janitor's boss." The findings were that if the children were asked nonleading questions, their responses were generally accurate both in terms of the facts and interpretation of the facts. However, if the questioning was leading, the researcher could manipulate most children to her interpretation of the event.

Although the ambiguous events in this study did not involve any body touch, the results have implications for cases involving body touch that may have either appropriate or abusive motivation. The findings suggest children might be persuaded that touch necessary for child care was sexual, or that sexual touch was necessary for child care.

RESEARCH ON PROGRAMMING

In addition, programming may lead to false positives for some children. Leichtman and Ceci (1995) studied two groups of children (3- to 4-year-olds and 5- to 6-year-olds) who had a brief exposure to Sam Stone, a stranger who came into their classroom. There were four different conditions, in which children received different types of information and/or questioning about Sam Stone and damage he might have done to a book and a teddy bear.

In the control condition, children received no information about Sam Stone before his appearance in the classroom and were questioned five times. In the first four sessions, they were asked to tell what they could remember about his visit, and in the last, they were asked directly whether he had done anything to the book or teddy bear. The vast majority of control children did not falsely accuse Sam Stone; furthermore, none of the older children's responses implicated Sam, and only 2.5% of responses of younger ones implicated him, when children were gently challenged.

Children in the second condition received four pre-visit indoctrination sessions in which they were told that Sam was messy and clumsy, and then the same four questioning sessions experienced by the control children. When they were subjected to a final "forensic" interview, no child made a false allegation in free-narrative accounts. However, 37% of intitial responses from younger children were that Sam had done one of these things, when shown these damaged items and asked direct questions about whether Sam was the culprit. Ten percent of their responses continued to be positive, when challenged. The rates for the older children were about half of those for the younger children.

In the third condition, children received no pre-event conditioning but four sessions of post-event suggestive questioning before the final interview. The suggestive questioning had similar effects to the stereotyping. For example, 12% of the younger children maintained Sam was the perpetrator, even when challenged about seeing him do it, and two of the older children said they had seen him commit these acts.

Finally, in the fourth condition children were subjected to the pre-visit indoctrination and four post-visit suggestive interviewing sessions. In their fifth interview, 72% of younger children and 38% of older ones initially said Sam was guilty of either ripping the book or soiling the teddy bear or both. Twenty-one percent of younger and about 11% of older children maintained they had seen one or both of these acts when challenged.

It is not altogether apparent what sort of real-life circumstance and questioning scenario this experiment is supposed to reflect. Because the staged event was in a preschool classroom, perhaps an allegation of abuse in day care was the analogue. However, in day care cases, pre-event programming is not found. In addition, the experiment is somewhat lacking in ecological validity because it does not involve harm to children, only to objects. Nevertheless, the study does indicate that children take what adults tell them seriously. Thus, if an adult characterizes a person in a certain way, children believe the adult. Similarly, if an adult communicates certain facts about a situation of which the child has no direct knowledge, the child will assume the adult is telling the truth.

Finally, there are two analogue studies that derive from the researchers' (Ceci, Huffman, Smith, & Loftus, 1994; Ceci, Loftus, Leichtman, & Bruck, n.d.) belief that therapists regularly have preschoolers imagine incidents of sexual abuse about which they have no memory, as a method of facilitating recollection during treatment. In one study, the children are encouraged to "think real hard," and in the other, to "make a picture in your head" in response to descriptions of real and fictitious experiences in the children's lives. In both studies, researchers interviewed parents to gather information about the real events, and then interviewers told the children that their parents had supplied information about things that had happened to them when they were younger.

The first study (Ceci, Huffman, Smith, & Loftus, 1994) involved 96 preschoolers, and the second (Ceci, Loftus, Leichtman, & Bruck, n.d.) 40 preschoolers. In both, the real and fictitious events included positive, neutral, and negative experiences. In the first study, children were told at the beginning that some of the events might not have happened, but were not told until the last session in the second. Children in the first group also received fewer programming sessions (7-10 versus 11) in which they were instructed to imagine the details of real and fictitious events.

Following several weeks of programming, children were interviewed and asked about each event. In both studies, children were highly accurate about actual experiences (85% to 100%). However, about a third of the children in the first study and 43% in the second gave false affirmations to fictitious events. The report from the first study does not differentiate among responses to positive, neutral, and negative events, but the second does. In the latter, false assents were the lowest for the negative events (falling off a tricycle and getting stitches), about 20%, and the highest for neutral, non-participant events (seeing someone at a bus stop), more than 60%. In both studies, younger children were more likely to give false assents than older ones, but patterns of individual children were fairly consistent over time. In the first study, Ceci and colleagues (1994) describe the resistance of three children making false assents to attempts to "deprogram" them.

Perhaps the most important finding from these studies is how many preschoolers are resistant to extensive programming by adults, especially as it relates to negative experiences (Everson, 1994). Moreover, apparently the children who did agree with the interviewer did not recount programmed events, but only agreed they had happened. Nevertheless, these studies do suggest that some young children can be programmed to believe they have had experiences they have not. To achieve this, the adult must go to considerable lengths, repeatedly asking the child to imagine the events. Because the literature on treatment of sexually abused children does not include recommendations to use guided imagery, the ecological validity of this study is questionable.

STUDY QUESTIONS

7. What role does positive reinforcement seem to play in the accuracy of children's reports?

8. How might the child's interpretation of events be affected by leading questions?

9. What does the research on programming indicate about the suggestibility of children?

10. What are the limitations of the research on child suggestibility?

In a different vein is a study by Saywitz and colleagues (1993). The goal of these researchers was to assist children in their accounts of events rather than to demonstrate their vulnerabilities. Over 100 children age 7 were involved in an experiment to test the effect of resistance training in decreasing vulnerability to misleading questions. The training was a cognitive-behavioral intervention consisting of teaching children to (a) identify leading questions, (b) mentally compare their memory to the response desired by the questioner, (c) give the correct answer if known, (d) answer "I don't know" or "I don't remember" if unknown, and (e) use self-talk to promote confidence, such as "I knew there would be questions like this." Children were trained in these strategies individually and in groups. The group training was more effective.

References

Brainerd, C., & Ornstein, P. (1991). Children's memory for witnessed events: The developmental backdrop. In J. Doris (Ed.), *The suggestibility of children's recollections*. Washington, DC: American Psychological Association.

Bruck, M., Ceci, S., Francoueur, E., & Renick, A. (1995). Anatomically detailed dolls do not facilitate preschoolers' reports of a pediatric examination involving genital touching. *Journal of Experimental Psychology: Applied, 1*(2), 95-109.

Carter, C., Bottoms, B., & Levine, M. (in press). Linguistic and socio-emotional influences on the accuracy of children's reports. *Law and Human Behavior.*

Ceci, S., Huffman, M., Smith, E., & Loftus, E. (1994). Repeatedly thinking about a non-event: Source misattributions among preschoolers. *Consciousness and Cognition, 3*, 388-407.

Ceci, S., Loftus, E., Leichtman, M., & Bruck, M. (n.d.). *The role of source misattributions in the creation of false beliefs among preschoolers.* (Available from Stephen Ceci, Department of Human Development, Cornell University, MVR Hall, Ithaca, NY 14853)

Clarke-Stewart, A., Thompson, W., & Lapore, S. (1989). Manipulating children's interpretations through interrogation. In G. Goodman (Chair), *Can children provide accurate eyewitness reports?* Symposium conducted at the biennial meeting of the Society for Research on Child Development, Kansas City, MO.

Doris, J. (Ed.). (1991). *The suggestibility of children's recollections*. Washington, DC: American Psychological Association.

Goodman, G., & Aman, C. (1990). Children's use of anatomically correct dolls to recount an event. *Child Development, 61*, 1859-1871.

Goodman, G., Bottoms, B., Schwartz-Kennedy, B., & Rudy, L. (1991). Children's memory for a stressful event: Improving children's reports. *Journal of Narrative and Life History, 1*, 9-99.

Goodman, G., & Clarke-Stewart, A. (1991). Suggestibility of children's testimony: Implications for sexual abuse investigations. In J. Doris (Ed.), *The suggestibility of children's recollections* (pp. 92-105). Washington, DC: American Psychological Association.

Goodman, G., Rudy, L., Bottoms, B., & Aman, C. (1990). Children's memory and children's concerns: Issues of ecological validity in the study of children's eyewitness testimony. In R. Fivush & J. Hudson (Eds.), *What young children remember and know*. New York: Cambridge University Press.

Goodman, G., Wilson, M., Hazan, C., & Reed, R. (1991). Children's memories of physical examinations that involve genital touch: Implications for reports of sexual abuse. *Journal of Clinical Psychology, 595*, 682-691.

Gordon, B., Ornstein, P., Nida, R., Follmer, A., Crenshaw, C., & Albert, G. (1993). Does the use of dolls facilitate children's memories of visits to the doctor? *Applied Cognitive Psychology, 7*, 459-474.

Leichtman, M., L. Ceci, S. (1995). The effects of stereotypes on pre-schoolers' reports. *Developmental Psychology, 31*(4), 568-578.

Lindberg, M. (1991). An interactive approach to assessing suggestibility and testimony of eyewitnesses. In J. Doris (Ed.), *The suggestibility of children's recollections* (pp. 47-55). Washington, DC: American Psychological Association,.

Loftus, E., & Davies, G. (1984). Distortions in the memory of children. *Journal of Social Issues, 40*(2), 51-67.

Perry, N., & Wrightsman, L. (1991). *The child witness.* Newbury Park, CA: Sage.

Peters, D. (1991). The influence of stress and arousal on the child witness. In J. Doris (Ed.), *The suggestibility of children's recollections* (pp. 60-76). Washington, DC: American Psychological Association.

Reed, D. (1993). Enhancing children's resistance to misleading questions during forensic interviews. *APSAC Advisor, 6*(2), 3-8.

Robin, M. (1991). *Assessing child maltreatment reports: The problem of false allegations.* New York: Haworth.

Saywitz, K., Goodman, G., & Myers, J. (1990, September). Can children provide accurate eyewitness reports? *Violence Update,* pp. 2, 4, 11.

Saywitz, K., Goodman, G., Nicholas, G., & Moan, S. (1989, April). *Children's memories of genital examinations: Implications for cases of child sexual assault.* Paper presented at the biennial meeting of the Society for Research on Child Development, Kansas City, MO.

Saywitz, K., Nathanson, R., Snyder, L., & Lamphear, V. (1993). *Preparing children for the investigative and judicial process: Improving communication, memory, and emotional resiliency* (Final report to the National Center on Child Abuse and Neglect). (Available from Karen Saywitz, Department of Psychiatry, UCLA School of Medicine, 1000 W. Carson St., Torrance, CA 90509)

Steward, M. (1989, November). *The development of a model interview for young child victims of sexual abuse* (Final report to the National Center on Child Abuse and Neglect). Davis: University of California, Davis, Department of Psychiatry.

Wakefield, H., & Underwager, R. (1988). *Accusations of child sexual abuse.* Springfield, IL: Charles C Thomas.

Zaragoza, M. (1991). Preschool children's susceptibility to memory impairment. In J. Doris (Ed.), *The suggestibility of children's recollections* (pp. 27-39). Washington, DC: American Psychological Association.

False Allegations

Almost every allegation of sexual abuse raises a question about its veracity. Although there has always been some skepticism about sexual abuse, many professionals working in this area perceive the current attitude as one of backlash. The truth of children's allegations of sexual abuse is being challenged, the techniques of professionals working in the sexual abuse field are being criticized, and the child protection system is being attacked for overdiagnosing sexual abuse as well as for other types of incompetence.

It is crucial for the professional involved in assessing children said to have been sexually abused to understand what is known about false allegations. Four topics will be discussed: the difference between an unsubstantiated case and a false one, criteria for deciding that a case is false, situations where there is risk that an allegation by an adult is false, and situations where there is risk that an allegation by a child is false.

Differentiating an Unsubstantiated Case From a False Allegation

In the United States, there are laws that mandate the reporting of suspected cases of child maltreatment, including suspected sexual abuse. Not only do state statutes require professionals (usually all persons in educational settings with children, all health care professionals, and all mental health personnel, and in some states, everyone regardless of the person's role) to report, but there are civil and criminal penalties for failure to report and protections from lawsuits for reporters.

Because the threshold for reporting is rather low (usually "reasonable cause to suspect maltreatment"), and there are legal protections and penalties, it should come as no surprise that nationally between 50% and 65% of reported cases are not substantiated (American Association for Protecting Children, 1988; McCurdy & Daro, 1994). Cases are not substantiated for a wide range of reasons.

Jones and McGraw (1987) studied the proportion of cases founded (substantiated) and reasons for failure to substantiate in a sample of 576 sexual abuse cases referred during 1983 to the Denver County Department of Social Services. In this sample, 53% of cases were founded, and the remaining 47% were not. The largest proportion were not founded because of insufficient information (24%), that is, the Department of Social Services could not make a determination because of the absence of incriminating or exculpatory evidence. The next largest category of cases was unsubstantiated suspicion. In these, usually an adult reported suspicion of sexual abuse and accepted the disposition of unfounded when it was rendered. Only 6% of cases were classified as fictitious. Of these, 1% were false allegations by children and 5% by adults. If the cases in which there was insufficient information are eliminated, the rates for fictitious allegations are 6% for adults and 2% for children. Although, as is noted below, these statistics have their limitations in that they are based on expert opinion rather than an irrefutable measure, they provide the best estimate to date of the rate of false reports.

Unfortunately, a number of authors (e.g., Gardner, 1991; Wexler, 1990), referring to the proportion of cases that are not substantiated, have irresponsibly implied that an unsubstantiated case is the equivalent of a false allegation (Besharov, 1985). Based on this distortion, these authors have asserted that there is an overwhelming flood of false, maliciously made reports of child maltreatment. For a careful review of the issue of overreporting of child abuse, see Finkelhor (1990).

As well, it has been asserted (Gardner, 1991; Renshaw, 1987, pp. 103-105; Wexler, 1990) that there is an atmosphere of hysteria about allegations of sexual abuse that is likened to the Salem witch trials. However, no data, but rather the authors' beliefs, are provided to support these assertions.

S T U D Y   Q U E S T I O N S

1. What are mandated reporting laws?
2. Nationally, what percentage of reported cases of child maltreatment are not substantiated?
3. What is the best estimate to date of the rate of false reports?

Methodology for Deciding an Allegation Is False

A fundamental obstacle to studying false allegations of sexual abuse is knowing with certainty that given cases are false and, therefore, knowing what the characteristics of false allegations are. The only way of knowing definitely that sexual abuse did not happen is that there was no opportunity, that is, that the offender did not have access to the victim or the victim was not exposed to the offender. A researcher would have to have a body of cases of this type, study them, and try to determine if these cases had any characteristics in common. Even then, it might be an error to assume that these characteristics are generally attributes of false allegations. In any case, no such research has been conducted.

Another approach might be to conduct analogue studies. However, one obstacle to such research is constructing ecologically valid scenarios. In most of the analogue studies conducted thus far, the numbers of false allegations are so small that deriving characteristics of false reports is difficult. However, researchers (Bruck et al., 1995; Ceci et al., in press; Goodman & Aman, 1990) found that younger children are less accurate and more suggestible than older ones.

Studying the characteristics of cases in which victims retract allegations does not appear to be an alternative because of the difficulty of determining which cases are true retractions of false allegations and which are false retractions of true allegations. A significant proportion of children recant in actual cases of sexual abuse (Goodwin, Sahd, & Rada, 1989; Sorenson & Snow, 1991), and indeed recantation is regarded as a characteristic of the child sexual abuse accommodation syndrome (Summit, 1983) and the dynamics associated with sexual abuse suggested by other authors (e.g., Sgroi, 1982).

Polygraph results have been used as one of several measures by one team of researchers (Raskin & Esplin, 1991). However, the scientific validity of the polygraph has yet to be demonstrated, and, indeed, in one series of studies it was found to have only a somewhat better than chance probability of differentiating true from false statements (Cross & Saxe, 1992; Saxe, Dougherty, & Cross, 1987).

In fact, what most researchers have used as strategies for identifying false allegations are (a) consensually arrived at criteria, (b) a disposition by a mandated professional, or (c) the author's clinical judgment. Although consensually arrived at criteria seem the most valid measure, experts can agree and all be wrong (Conte et al., 1991; Faller & Corwin, 1995). For example, for over 50 years, based on Freud's work, mental health professionals believed that the overwhelming majority of children's accusations of sexual abuse had their basis in fantasy (Faller & Corwin, 1995).

There are two large-scale studies examining the issue of false allegations, that of Jones and McGraw (1987), and one sponsored by the Association of Family and Conciliation Courts (Thoennes & Tjaden, 1990). Their criteria for determining an allegation to be untrue or probably untrue will be discussed.

Jones and McGraw (1987) first asked caseworkers to categorize cases (categories, as already noted, included fictitious allegation by child and fictitious allegation by adult). If there was a question about how to categorize the case, it was reviewed by the researchers and classified. However, there was also a review of other cases by the research team. It appears that 10 randomly selected cases from the categories of reliable accounts, insufficient evidence, and unsubstantiated suspicion were reviewed and complete agreement was found between the caseworkers and the researchers. It also appears that all cases where there were recantations, fictitious allegations by adults, and fictitious allegations by children were examined by the research team, and a number of the fictitious allegation cases were reclassified.

Thoennes and Tjaden (1990) studied allegations of sexual abuse in divorce. They surveyed 9,000 cases in family/divorce courts involving custody/visitation disputes from 12 juridictions to arrive at a sample 169 cases (less than 2%) where there were allegations of sexual abuse. In their study, to determine the likelihood of sexual abuse, they employed the disposition of the child protection worker and/or the conclusion of a court-appointed evaluator. Cases were classified likely (50%), unlikely (33%), and inconclusive (17%). Cases where there was disagreement between the child protection worker and the court-appointed evaluator, as well as other cases without a definitive disposition, were classified as inconclusive.

The remaining studies, which mostly consist of small samples from the practices of the authors, either do not articulate the criteria employed or rely on the clinical judgment of the authors (Benedek & Schetky, 1985; Faller, 1991; Goodwin, Sahd, & Rada, 1980; Green, 1986). Generally, information relied on includes not only the child's statements and behavior but also information related to the parents and the circumstances of the allegation. There are also authors who describe what they believe are the characteristics of false allegations but provide no data (Blush & Ross, 1986; Gardner, 1989; Renshaw, 1987, pp. 301-303).

One of the problems is that a criterion that might indicate a false allegation for one author could be regarded as insignificant or even indicative of a true account for another. For example, Green (1986) reported on 11 cases involving custody disputes he had seen in his practice. He opined that four of these accounts were false, and from them derived characteristics of false allegations, which he asserted were especially prevalent in divorce. His article occasioned an article in response by a number of leading experts in sexual abuse, Corwin, Berliner, Goodman, Goodwin, and White (1987), which challenged his list of characteristics of false allegations, and among other things pointed out that divorce was both a context where ongoing sexual abuse might finally be reported and a situation that might precipitate sexual abuse. Similarly, the practice of making inferences about the likelihood of sexual abuse from behaviors during interactions between the child and the accused parent has been challenged (Faller, Froning, & Lipovsky, 1991).

Illustrative of the fallibility of clinical judgment about the truth of an account of abuse is the report from Leichtman & Ceci (1995) related to the Sam Stone study, described in Chapter 9. They showed videotapes of three children from the study to professional audiences at two conferences. These professionals scored at less than chance level regarding the veracity of children's accounts. Comparable findings regarding human error were made by Dahlberg (1992). She had mothers of 97 children assist them in developing either a true or false account of physical punishment by another adult. She then had the children's videotaped statements rated for veracity by graduate students, probation officers, social workers, and licensure applicants. They were able to correctly classify 52% of the accounts. Their assessments were compared to those of the computer, using 31 objective criteria. The computer was correct 84% of the time. These studies argue in favor of criteria that are systematically applied and against relying on subjective impressions of truthfulness.

In contrast to the almost insurmountable difficulty of determining for sure that an allegation is false, it is possible to know that in certain cases the allegation is true. For example, in instances where the offender confesses, where there is a reliable eyewitness, where pornography involving the victim is found, where the offender's DNA-typed semen is detected, where the child is diagnosed with venereal disease, or where there is other compelling physical evidence, evaluators can be virtually certain that sexual abuse occurred. However, the absence of these compelling findings does not mean that the accusation is false.

There have been four studies of children's statements in cases substantiated by other means (e.g., a confession, physical evidence, an eyewitness; Faller, 1988b; Lawson & Chaffin, 1992; Sorenson & Snow, 1991; Terry, 1991). These studies have found that children do not necessarily give complete and coherent accounts of their victimization, despite the veracity of the allegation. Sorenson and Snow (1991) examined 116 cases with other means of substantiation and found that 72% of children initially denied sexual abuse and 78% at first gave a tentative disclosure. Terry (1991) examined the accounts of sexual abuse of 18 children victimized by a single offender who confessed. He found that on average the children recounted less than 80% of the activities mentioned by the offender. Faller (1988b) examined children's statements and behavior in clinical assessments for 103 cases where offenders gave some level of confession. Although each of the three general criteria assumed to be characteristic of a true allegation was found in about 80% of cases, she found that only 68% of children's accounts contained all three clinical criteria. Lawson and Chaffin (1992) reviewed the records of 28 children, ages 3 through menarche, diagnosed as having venereal disease and subsequently interviewed by an expert in child assessment. Fifty-seven percent did not indicate the source of their venereal disease, and 83% of children whose parent was unsupportive failed to disclose.

Thus, it appears that clinical interviews, even when conducted by sexual abuse experts, are likely to yield false negatives, that is, a failure to disclose actual sexual abuse, or less than complete disclosure, in a substantial number of cases. This appears to be a problem of larger proportions than false positives, that is, false accusations of sexual abuse by children.

To summarize, it is important to appreciate that it is quite difficult to be sure that allegations are false. Hence, the conclusions one can draw from studies of false allegations are limited, because they could include some true cases. Moreover, although it is possible in some cases to be sure sexual abuse has happened, studies of these cases suggest that the clinical characteristics of the child's account, generally relied on in instances without other means of substantiation, are not found in all valid cases. A more detailed discussion of these clinical criteria is provided in the section on criteria for substantiating sexual abuse.

STUDY QUESTIONS

4. What are the fundamental obstacles to studying false allegations of sexual abuse?

   a. Discuss the spectrum of opinion regarding recantation.

   b. Discuss the spectrum of opinion regarding the relationship between divorce and allegations of sexual abuse.

   c. What is known about the fallibility of clinical judgment in evaluating allegations of sexual abuse?

5. When is it possible to know for sure that an allegation is true? Does the absence of such findings indicate a false allegation?

6. What is known about the nature of children's statements in cases substantiated by other means?

7. Do clinical interviews seem more likely to yield false negatives or false positives?

False Allegations by Adults

The limited research that compares the proportion of false allegations generated by adults and children indicates adults are more likely to make such allegations than children. For example, Jones and McGraw (1987) found adults three times (6% of reports, when insufficient-information cases are eliminated) more likely to make fictitious allegations than children (2% of reports, when insufficient-information cases are eliminated).

Adults in certain contexts are reported to be more likely to make false allegations of sexual abuse. The context cited most frequently is divorce (Benedek & Schetky, 1985; Faller, 1991; Gardner, 1989, 1991; Jones & McGraw, 1987; Klajner-Diamond, Wehrspann, & Steinhauer, 1987). However, there is disagreement regarding the motivations for making false allegations. Benedek and Schetky (1985) and Gardner (1989) find that these parents, almost all of whom they say are mothers, make calculated false reports. Gardner describes these women as wanting to "wreak vengeance" on their ex-spouses. However, Benedek and Schetky also give a large percentage of these mothers the diagnosis of paranoid personality.

Others have found few consciously made false allegations. Jones and McGraw (1987) noted that a substantial number of adults making fictitious allegations were suffering from posttraumatic stress disorder (PTSD) and that a number were otherwise psychiatrically disturbed. In these cases, untrue reports were not conniving, but a consequence of psychiatric illness. Thoennes and Tjaden (1990) had data on motivation of only half of the accusers in their 169 cases, but found only 8 cases where the report appeared to be a calculated false accusation and 5 where the charge appeared to arise from parental emotional disturbance. In only half of their cases was the accusation of sexual abuse made by the mother. Faller (1991), in a study of 136 cases with sexual abuse allegations in divorce, found that in the 15% of cases where the allegation appeared false, most wrongly accusing parents seemed to genuinely believe the child had been victimized. Only three parents appeared to knowingly make false charges, and two of these were fathers. Other dynamics identified by Faller in divorce-related allegations were (a) disclosure of sexual abuse precipitates divorce, (b) divorce precipitates disclosure of sexual abuse, and (c) divorce precipitates sexual abuse.

Emotional disturbance, other than in divorce cases, also appears to be a problem that can cause an adult to incorrectly believe that a child has been sexually abused. Goodwin, Sahd, and Rada (1980), Klajner-Diamond and colleagues (1987), and Faller (1988a) found that sometimes, psychotic adults have delusions that children are being sexually abused. And some of the adults in Jones and McGraw's sample were not involved in divorces, but suffered from PTSD and other psychiatric disturbance. Interestingly, two of their nine fictitious accusers were disturbed professionals. Klajner-Diamond and colleagues report PTSD in some mothers who make false allegations, although they have also had experience with mothers with PTSD whose children had, in fact, been sexually abused.

In contrast to these observations that false allegations are made, but in limited circumstances and often by disturbed individuals, is the work of

Gardner (1991, 1992), who asserts that as a society we are preoccupied with sexual abuse and pronounces a "sex abuse hysteria." Although he says that he believes that 95% of allegations are true, he declares that the overwhelming majority of allegations involving day care, nursery schools, and divorces are false. He faults parents, "validators," and "therapists" (his quotes). He attributes the deluge of what he says are false accusations essentially to the wish of parents and professionals themselves to be involved in sexual activities with children. According to him, making false allegations of sexual abuse and viewing sexual abuse as a rampant phenomenon satisfy the perverse needs of the accuser, because every time the person makes such an accusation she or he imagines the sexual activity and is sexually gratified by this fantasy. As well, he asserts that the overwhelming majority of persons conducting evaluations of cases of sexual abuse and providing sexual abuse treatment are incompetent. As mentioned earlier, despite his statement that he has 30 years of experience as a psychiatrist, Gardner provides no data to support his opinions. Indeed, he scorns those who cite research to support their views.

STUDY QUESTIONS

8. Do adults seem to be more or less likely than children to make false allegations of sexual abuse?

9. In what contexts do adults seem to be more likely to make false allegations? In divorce-related allegations, what other dynamics may be operating?

10. Discuss the spectrum of opinion regarding adult motivations for making false allegations of sexual abuse. What role does emotional disturbance seem to play?

11. What research does Gardner offer to support his opinions regarding the supposed "sex abuse hysteria"?

False Allegations by Children

As already noted, false accusations of sexual abuse by children are quite uncommon (e.g., Levanthal, Bentovim, Elton, Tranter, & Read, 1987). Jones and McGraw (1987) found they comprised 1% of all reports (and 2% when insufficient-information cases are eliminated). Faller (1988a) believed that

3% of her clinical sample of 194 cases were false accounts by children. Goodwin and colleagues (1980) found one false account by a child in the 46 cases they reviewed. Horowitz, Gomes-Schwartz, and Sauzier (1984), whose project in the Department of Psychiatry at Tufts University involved extensive assessment, found less that 5% of 181 consecutive referrals to be untrue.

Reports indicate most false accusations are made by older children, usually by adolescents. Jones and McGraw identified eight allegations made by five children, four of whom were female adolescents who had been sexually abused in the past and had symptoms of PTSD. These researchers concluded that the PTSD resulted in distortions leading to the false allegations. Faller (1988a) also identified adolescents as making the majority of false allegations. These children had histories of prior sexual abuse, but appeared to make the allegations for instrumental reasons, for example, to cover up their consensual sexual activity or to effect removal from the home. Benedek and Schetky (1987a, 1987b) similarly report false accusations made by adolescents for secondary gain. The AACAP guidelines (1990) also caution evaluators that adolescents may make false reports because of vindictiveness or to cover their own sexuality. The majority of the false reports in Horowitz and colleagues' (1984) sample were from adolescents as well. Reasons they noted were anger at the accused, an attempt to influence living situation, and emotional disturbance.

Very young children may also be the source of false or possibly fictitious allegations (Levanthal et al., 1987). Faller (1988a, 1993) has identified social desirability responses as another category of false allegation by young children. Young children may not understand the question or may merely wish to please the evaluator and respond affirmatively to yes-no questions (e.g., "Did Uncle Joe put his finger in your peepee?"). This possibility is the reason for limiting the use of yes-no questions. Boat and Everson (1988), Reed (1993), and White and Quinn (1988) also express strong reservations regarding these sorts of questions. However, as noted earlier, the analogue studies employing yes-no questions find them only rarely to result in false positives (Goodman & Clarke-Stewart, 1991).

Children whose parents are involved in divorce with custody or visitation disputes have also been described by a number of authors as making false accusations (Benedek & Schetky, 1987a, 1987b; Gardner, 1989; Green, 1986; Jones & McGraw, 1987; Jones & Seig, 1988; Levanthal et al., 1987; Renshaw, 1987, pp. 301-303; Wakefield & Underwager, 1988). Jones and McGraw describe nine cases seen at the Kempe Center, all involving custody disputes, where both parent and child made a false allegation. They noted enmeshed relationships between these parents and children, and, as cited earlier, psychiatric disturbance in the parents.

In their study of 212 sexual abuse experts, Conte and colleagues (1991) found 90% of respondents thought that being involved in a custody battle "occasionally" resulted in distortions of the child's report. Conte and colleagues also note that a majority of professionals responding to their survey thought that psychological disturbance of the child, being exposed to a sexually overstimulating but nonabusive atmosphere, wanting to punish a hated parent, having no sense of obligation to tell the truth, and being too young to distinguish fact from fantasy could lead to distortions in children's reports. However, respondents most commonly rated these conditions as seldom occurring. (See also Robin [1991] and Yuille, Tymofievich, & Maxey [1995] for comparable categorizations of false accounts by children.)

Children have also been noted to very occasionally identify the wrong abuser. Faller (1988a) has noted children to cite someone who is less feared or less loved than the actual offender and has found four children in 136 divorce cases accusing their biological fathers when in fact someone else committed the abuse (Faller, 1991). However, De Young (1986) is of the opinion that the evidence is against the child implicating a convenient person rather than the actual person.

Finally, Gardner (1991), again in contrast to the opinions of other professionals, cites the following factors as leading to false allegations of sexual abuse by children: their polymorphous perversity and consequent penchant to fantasize about sexual activity, including such activity with adults; children's exposure to sexual abuse prevention programs, which causes them to confuse appropriate touch with sexual abuse and stimulate their sexual fantasies; and the "ubiquity of environmental sexual stimuli," such as MTV (rock music videos) and pornographic videotapes.

STUDY QUESTIONS

12. Approximately what percentage of all sexual abuse reports appear to be false allegations by children?

13. Which age group is most likely to make a false allegation? What reasons have been noted for these allegations?

14. In what contexts might young children make false allegations, or sometimes identify the wrong abuser?

References

American Academy of Child and Adolescent Psychiatry (AACAP). (1990, December). *Guidelines for the evaluation of child and adolescent sexual abuse.* (Available from AACAP, 3615 Wisconsin Ave. N.W., Washington, DC 20016)

American Association for Protecting Children. (1988). *Highlights of official child neglect and abuse reporting.* Denver: American Humane Association.

Benedek, E., & Schetky, D. (1985). Allegations of child sexual abuse in custody cases. In E. Benedek & D. Schetky (Eds.), *Advances in child psychiatry and the law* (pp. 145-156). New York: Brunner/Mazel.

Benedek, E., & Schetky, D. (1987a). Problems in validating allegations of sexual abuse: Part 1. Factors affecting perception and recall of events. *Journal of the American Academy of Child and Adolescent Psychiatry, 26,* 912-915.

Benedek, E., & Schetky, D. (1987b). Problems in validating allegations of sexual abuse: Part 2. Clinical evaluation. *Journal of the American Academy of Child and Adolescent Psychiatry, 26,* 916-921.

Besharov, D. (1985). Doing something about child abuse. *Harvard Journal of Law and Public Policy, 8*(3), 539-566.

Blush, G., & Ross, K. (1986). *SAID syndrome: Sexual allegations in divorce.* Unpublished manuscript. (Available from G. Blush, Ed.D., Macomb County Psychodiagnostic Clinic, Mt. Clemens, MI)

Boat, B., & Everson, M. (1988). The use of anatomical dolls among professionals in sexual abuse evaluations. *Child Abuse & Neglect, 12,* 171-179.

Bruck, M., Ceci, S., Francoueur, E., & Renick, A. (1995). Anatomically detailed dolls do not facilitate preschoolers' reports of a pediatric examination involving genital touching. *Journal of Experimental Psychology: Applied, 1*(2), 95-109.

Conte, J., Sorenson, E., Fogarty, L., & Dalla Rosa, J. (1991). Evaluating children's reports of sexual abuse: Results from a survey of professionals. *American Journal of Orthopsychiatry, 61,* 428-437.

Corwin, D., Berliner, L., Goodman, G., Goodwin, J., & White, S. (1987). Child sexual abuse in custody disputes: No easy answers. *Journal of Interpersonal Violence, 2,* 91-105.

Cross, T., & Saxe, L. (1992). A critique of the validity of polygraph testing in child sexual abuse cases. *Journal of Child Abuse, 143,* 19-33.

Dahlberg, C. (1992, January). *True and false allegations of physical abuse: The role of the mother in constructing a believable story.* Paper presented at the Conference on the Health Science Response to Child Maltreatment, San Diego, CA.

De Young, M. (1986). A conceptual model for judging the truthfulness of a young child's allegation of sexual abuse. *American Journal of Orthopsychiatry, 56,* 550-558.

Faller, K. C. (1988a). *Child sexual abuse: An interdisciplinary manual for diagnosis, case management, and treatment.* New York: Columbia University Press.

Faller, K. C. (1988b). Criteria for judging the credibility of children's statements about their sexual abuse. *Child Welfare, 67,* 389-401.

Faller, K. C. (1991). Possible explanations for allegation of sexual abuse in divorce. *American Journal of Orthopsychiatry, 61,* 86-91.

Faller, K. C. (1993). *Child sexual abuse: Assessment and intervention issues.* Washington, DC: U.S. Department of Health and Human Services, National Center on Child Abuse and Neglect.

Faller, K. C., & Corwin, D. (1995). Children's interview statements and behaviors: Professional consensus and research findings for the identification of sexually abused children. *Child Abuse & Neglect, 19,* 71-82.

Faller, K. C., Froning, M., & Lipovsky, J. (1991). The parent-child interview: Use in evaluating child allegations of sexual abuse by a parent. *American Journal of Orthopsychiatry, 61,* 552-557.

Finkelhor, D. (1990, Winter). Is child abuse overreported? *Public Welfare,* pp. 23-29.

Gardner, R. (1989). Differentiating between bona fide and fabricated allegations of sexual abuse of children. *Journal of the American Academy of Matrimonial Lawyers, 5,* 1-25.

Gardner, R. (1991). *The sex abuse hysteria: The Salem witch trials revisited.* Cresskill, NJ: Creative Therapeutics.

Gardner, R. (1992). *True and false accusations of child sex abuse.* Cresskill, NJ: Creative Therapeutics.

Goodman, G., & Aman, C. (1990). Children's use of anatomically correct *dolls. Child Development, 61,* 1859-1871.

Goodman, G. & Clark-Stewart, A. (1991). Suggestibility in children's testimony: Implications for sexual abuse investigations. In J. Doris (Ed.), *The suggestibility of children's recollections* (pp. 92-105). Washington, DC: American Psychological Association.

Goodwin, J., Sahd, D., & Rada, R. (1980). Incest hoax. In W. Holder (Ed.), *Sexual abuse of children* (pp. 37-45.). Englewood, CO: American Humane Association.

Goodwin, J., Sahd, D., & Rada, R. (1989). False accusations and false denials of incest: Clinical myths and clinical realities. In J. Goodwin (Ed.), *Sexual abuse: Incest victims and their families* (pp. 19-36). Boston: John Wright.

Green, A. (1986). True and false allegations of sexual abuse in child custody disputes. *Journal of the American Academy of Child and Adolescent Psychiatry, 25,* 449-456.

Horowitz, J., Gomes-Schwartz, B., & Sauzier, M. (1984). Unconfirmed cases of sexual abuse. In Tufts New England Medical Center, Division of Child Psychiatry, *Sexually exploited children: Service and research project* (Final report for the Office of Juvenile Justice and Delinquency Prevention). Washington, DC.

Jones, D., & McGraw, E. M. (1987). Reliable and fictitious accounts of sexual abuse to children. *Journal of Interpersonal Violence, 2,* 27-45.

Jones, D., & Seig, A. (1988). Child sexual abuse allegations in custody and visitation cases: A report of 20 cases. In B. Nicholson & J. Bulkley (Eds.), *Sexual abuse allegations in custody and visitation cases* (pp. 22-31). Washington, DC: American Bar Association.

Klajner-Diamond, H., Wehrspann, W., & Steinhauer, P. (1987). Assessing the credibility of young children's allegations of sexual abuse: Clinical issues. *Canadian Journal of Psychiatry, 32,* 610-614.

Lawson, L., & Chaffin, M. (1992). False negatives in sexual abuse disclosure interviews. *Journal of Interpersonal Violence, 7,* 532-542.

Levanthal, J., Bentovim, A., Elton, A., Tranter, M., & Read, L. (1987). What to ask when sexual abuse is suspected. *Archives of Disease in Childhood, 62,* 1188-1195.

Leichtman, M., & Ceci, S. The effects of stereotypes and suggestions on preschoolers reports. *Developmental Psychology, 31*(4), 568-578.

McCurdy, K., & Daro, D. (1994, April). *Current trends in child abuse reporting and fatalities: Results of the 1993 annual Fifty State Survey.* Chicago: National Committee for the Prevention of Child Abuse.

Raskin, D., & Esplin, P. (1991). Assessment of children's statements of sexual abuse. In J. Doris (Ed.), *The suggestibility of children's recollections* (pp. 153-164). Washington, DC: American Psychological Association.

Reed, D. (1993). Enchancing children's resisitance to misleading questions during forensic interviews. *APSAC Advisor, 6*(2), 3-8.

Renshaw, D. (1987). Child sexual abuse: When wrongly charged. In *Encyclopedia Britannica: Medical and health annual.* Chicago: Encyclopedia Britannica.

Robin, M. (1991). *Assessing child maltreatment reports: The problem of false allegations.* New York: Haworth.

Saxe, L., Dougherty, D., & Cross, T. (1987). The validity of polygraph testing: Scientific analysis and public controversy. In L. S. Wrightsman, C. E. Willis, & S. M. Kassin (Eds.), *On the witness stand: Controversies in the courtroom* (pp. 14-36). Newbury Park, CA: Sage.

Sgroi, S. (1982). *Handbook of clinical intervention in child sexual abuse.* Lexington, MA: Lexington Books.

Sorenson, T., & Snow, B. (1991). How children tell: The process of disclosure in child sexual abuse. *Child Welfare, 70,* 3-15.

Summit, R. (1983). The child sexual abuse accommodation syndrome. *Child Abuse & Neglect, 9,* 177-193.

Terry, W. (1991, January). *Perpetrator and victim accounts of sexual abuse.* Paper presented at the Conference on the Health Science Response to Child Maltreatment, San Diego, CA. (Available from William Terry, M.D., 343 N. Allumbaugh St., Boise, ID 83704)

Thoennes, N., & Tjaden, P. (1990). The extent, nature, and validity of sexual abuse allegations in custody/visitation disputes. *Child Abuse & Neglect, 14,* 151-163.

Wakefield, H., & Underwager, R. (1988). *Accusations of child sexual abuse.* Springfield, IL: Charles C Thomas.

Wexler, R. (1990). *Wounded innocents: The real victims of the war against child abuse.* Buffalo, NY: Prometheus.

White, S., & Quinn. K. (1988). Investigatory independence in child sexual abuse evaluations: Conceptual considerations. *Bulletin of the American Academy of Psychiatry and the Law, 16,* 269-278.

Yuille, J. (1995). The nature of allegations of child sexual abuse. In T. Ney (Ed.), *True and false allegations of child sexual abuse* (pp. 21-46). New York: Brunner/Mazel.

Criteria for Deciding
Whether an Allegation Is Valid

Basic Reference

Faller, K. C. (1993). *Child sexual abuse: Assessment and intervention issues.* Washington, DC: U.S. Department of Health and Human Services, National Center on Child abuse and Neglect.

This manual, cited earlier, was prepared for the National Center on Child Abuse and Neglect. It includes a discussion of strategies for determining whether sexual abuse has occurred.

Review and Critique

A major clinical and forensic challenge in the sexual abuse field is making a decision about the veracity of an allegation. We have progressed from a time when clinicians responded quite intuitively or used their own personal criteria. In fact, a number of authors have written about this topic and proposed criteria for making decisions about the validity of sexual abuse allegations. Twelve such guidelines were found. These works will be reviewed, and commonalities and differences in their criteria will be charted and discussed.

The Guidelines

Sgroi, Porter, and Blick (1982) were among the first professionals to offer guidance about deciding if a child has been sexually abused. They focus on behavioral indicators of both a sexual and nonsexual nature in the child. They list 20 such indicators:

1. Overly compliant behavior
2. Acting-out, aggressive behavior
3. Pseudomature behavior
4. Hints about sexual activity
5. Persistent and inappropriate sexual play with peers or toys or with themselves, or sexually aggressive behavior with others
6. Detailed and age-inappropriate understanding of sexual behavior (especially by young children)
7. Arriving early at school and leaving late
8. Poor peer relationships or inability to make friends
9. Lack of trust
10. Nonparticipation in school or social activities
11. Inability to concentrate in school
12. Sudden drop in school performance
13. Extraordinary fears of males
14. Seductive behavior with males
15. Running away from home
16. Sleep disturbances
17. Regressive behavior
18. Withdrawal
19. Clinical depression
20. Suicidal feelings

Sgroi et al.'s book is a pioneering effort to isolate characteristics of sexually abused children that might be noted during the course of validation. Today, clinicians would regard the sexual indicators as more likely to be associated with sexual abuse and would recognize that nonsexual indicators could be related to a wide range of trauma, including sexual abuse.

Faller (1984, 1988, 1990, 1993) has addressed the decision-making issue in several writings. Her protocol includes interview data and corroborating information. Interview data are subsumed under three general categories: (a) statements and/or behavior regarding the sexual acts, which are explicit, told from a child's viewpoint, and demonstrate advanced sexual knowledge; (b) information regarding the context of the abuse, such as when, where, and under what circumstances the abuse occurred; and (c) an emotional reaction consistent with the account given, for example, reluctance to disclose, fear, anxiety, or anger. Corroborating evidence includes the following: confessions, medical findings, physical evidence, and eyewitnesses. The clinical protocol is derived from the research on 103 confessed cases (Faller, 1988).

De Young (1986) observes that it is rare for a young child's account of sexual abuse to be characterized by "clarity," "celerity," "certainty," and "consistency" and cites the reasons for the absence of such findings. She then sets out criteria for judging the truthfulness of an allegation. First, she states that the evaluator should probe for elaborated details, which should include (a) a description of a specific action (sexual abuse), (b) the context of the abuse, (c) secrecy details, and (d) affective details, that is, how the child felt at the time of the abuse. Second, she sees sexual and nonsexual behavioral indicators as important, but notes that lists of such indicators are taken from a variety of contexts and are a "melange." She suggests using the four categories of effects of sexual abuse developed by Finkelhor and Browne (Finkelhor, 1986): traumatic sexualization, betrayal, disempowerment, and stigmatization. She then instructs the evaluator to assess the vulnerability of the child to sexual abuse, and finally any motivation for lying.

Levanthal collaborated with British colleagues Bentovim, Elton, Tranter, and Read in developing a framework for use in medical settings (Levanthal et al., 1987). Having noted that false allegations by children are rare, they set forth the following criteria for substantiation: (a) the child's attitude during disclosure, (b) detail related to both the sexual abuse and context, (c) a description of any threats regarding secrecy, and (d) the child's response to telling the doctor.

Sink (1988) proposes a hierarchical model for evaluation of possible sexual abuse, with four levels. She notes that there is a difference between legal criteria and psychosocial criteria for validating an allegation. Level 1 satisfies legal requirements and is labeled direct communication. It is defined as verbal disclosure, demonstrations with anatomical dolls, and physical corroboration.

Level 2 consists of indirect communication, such as ambiguous statements, sexualized play, behavior, content in response to projective measures, and reactions to sexual stimuli, or retraction of prior disclosure. Level 3 is acute traumatic symptomatology, which lacks sexualized content, found in the child's play or functioning (e.g., sleep disturbances, toileting problems). Level 4 is cumulative stress symptomatology, which is manifested in chronic behavioral maladaptation, such as phobias, depression, or conduct disorder.

Corwin (1988) centers his discussion on the child's emotional and behavioral indicators, categorized into three levels of specificity, or levels of likelihood that the criteria indicate sexual abuse. These vary somewhat by developmental stage, that is, whether the child is a preschooler, school aged, or an adolescent. The general categories of indicators most specific to sexual abuse for all developmental stages are (a) nightmares about the sexual abuse; (b) premature eroticization; (c) fearfulness related to sexuality, the sexual abuse situation, or the alleged offender; (d) an age-appropriate, circumstantially congruent description of being sexually abused; and (e) dissociative phenomena. These indicators were developed and refined by a group of experts in clinical evaluation of sexual abuse.

Jones and McGraw (1987) developed a list of attributes of the child's statement indicating a true allegation: (a) explicit detail, (b) unique or distinguishing detail, (c) child's language, (d) child's perspective, and (e) emotion expressed. Other information from the child is also important: (a) the child's psychological response to the abuse, (b) the pattern of abuse, (c) an element of secrecy, and in some cases, (d) pornography, sadism, and ritualism. They also include "supporting features" in their criteria. These are (a) a family history that includes problems that are correlated with sexual abuse, such as spouse abuse, substance abuse, or criminal activity; (b) symptomatic behavior of the child during the time of the abuse; (c) the pattern of disclosure; (d) the child's statements to other people; (e) consistency in the child's account; (f) expression of sexual themes play or drawings; (g) advanced sexual knowledge, and (h) other victims within the household. Physical or physiological evidence is an additional criterion.

Conte and colleagues (1991), in their survey of 212 sexual abuse experts from 44 states, inquired, among other things, about criteria used in substantiating a report and the level of importance of each criterion. The highest ranked criterion was compelling medical evidence. This was followed by a number of attributes related to sexuality and characteristics of the child's statement. Those related to sexuality were (a) age-inappropriate sexual knowledge, (b) sexualized play during the interview, (c) precocious or apparently seductive behavior, (d) response to the anatomical dolls consistent with that of a sexually abused child, (e) excessive masturbation, and (f) preoccupation with the genitals. The highly rated characteristics of the child's account are (a) consistency over time, (b) idiosyncratic details surrounding the abuse, (c) a progression of sexual activity, (d) elements of pressure or coercion, (e) a logical account, and (f) the ability to distinguish fact from fantasy. The authors are justifiably critical of respondents for giving high ratings to some of these criteria, because in some instances no empirical studies can be cited to support their importance, and in others, situations of sexual abuse can readily be cited where the criteria would not be found. An interpretation of the responses to their questionnaire may be that the presence of these criteria is supportive of a true allegation of sexual abuse, but their absence should not lead to the conclusion that no sexual abuse occurred.

Benedek and Schetky (1987a, 1987b) list findings related to the child that enhance and detract from the credibility of the allegation. The areas in which they present criteria include (a) language, (b) spontaneous play/drawings, (c) affect, (d) behavior, (e) motives, (f) memory, (g) cognitive development, (h) credibility history, (i) physical exam, and (j) relationship with parents.

Wehrspann and colleagues (1987; Klajner-Diamond, Wehrspann, & Steinhauer, 1987)) divide confirming findings into two general categories, medical indicators and criteria from the child's presentation. The latter may include information from the validating interview and information provided from others who have contact with the child. The criteria are (a) spontaneity; (b) repetitions over time; (c) internal consistency; (d) external consistency; (e) embedded responses (remarks, usually made in the context of conversation about something else, which indicate advanced sexual knowledge, memories of sexual abuse, or affect arising from the sexual abuse); (f) amount/quality of details; (g) story told from a child's viewpoint; (h) evidence of the (child sexual abuse) accommodation syndrome, or conversely, (i) consistency in the face of challenge; and (j) sexually specific symptoms.

Wehrspann and colleagues also attempt to compare their criteria to those advanced by others, especially the German clinicians (Undeutch, 1989), whose work guided that of Raskin and Esplin (1991) and Yuille (1988) described below. Although they generally find agreement about criteria, their work preceded much of the current writing on this topic.

Raskin and Esplin (1991), Stellar and Boychuk (1992), and Yuille (1988) espouse a method of evaluating the truthfulness of children's statements about their sexual abuse called criteria-based content analysis (CBCA), which has its origins in Germany (Undeutch, 1989). CBCA requires a careful examination of the child's spontaneous statement, either using a videotape of the child interview or a transcript. The technique analyzes 19 content areas, which are organized into five general categories. The categories and content areas are as follows: (a) general characteristics (logical structure, unstructured production, and quantity of details); (b) specific contents (contextual embedding, descriptions of interactions, reproduction of conversation, and unexpected complications); (c) peculiarities of content (unusual details, superfluous details, accurately reported details misunderstood, related external associations, accounts of subjective mental state, and attribution of perpetrator's mental state); (d) motivation (spontaneous corrections, admitting lack of memory, raising doubts about one's testimony, self-deprecation, and pardoning the perpetrator); and (e) offense-specific elements (details characteristic of the offense). The content areas suggest that this methodology is potentially more useful with older than younger children. In addition, unlike the other schemas, this one does not have criteria specific to sexual abuse.

Raskin and Esplin (1991) and Stellar and Boychuk (1992) report on research using CBCA in an analogue study in Germany and in a study involving children seen by Raskin and Esplin, 20 of whom CBCA found to be sexually abused and 20 of whom CBCA found were not, that is, whose statements were doubtful. Thus, like the protocol developed by Faller, CBCA has a small amount of research to support its validity. However, CBCA is frequently used by its proponents, not as a method for substantiating an allegation of sexual abuse, but as a strategy to challenge the conclusions of other mental health professionals, both in terms of their methodology and amount and type of information elicited from the child.

Heiman (1992) reviews past attempts to develop frameworks for decision making about sexual abuse. Her goal is to present a schema that can assist the clinician in organizing the assessment process and in decision making. She divides the areas for data gathering into five domains: (a) history of symptoms, both sexual (inappropriate or precocious sexual behavior, intrusive recollections of the abuse) and nonsexual (e.g., sleep disturbance, aggressive behavior, clinging behavior, exaggerated fears, somatic complaints, dissociation); (b) (child's) verbal report (explicit details, details beyond the child's developmental stage, a progression of activities, secrecy, threats, bribes, contextual information, affective details, and idiosyncratic details); (c) phenomenological experience of abuse (as stated or evidenced in the form of sequelae, such as feelings of betrayal, powerlessness, stigmatization, and shame and guilt); (d) presentational style (e.g., affect, evidence of coaching); and (e) corroborating evidence (e.g., medical findings, police evidence, statements to others, other witnesses). For each area, she poses framing questions and lists indicators for positive findings. She argues for systematic consideration of findings in all five domains, but like other authors, does not offer any minimum criteria for a positive finding of sexual abuse.

Gardner (1987, 1989) and Green (1986) have also produced criteria for differentiating true from false allegations of sexual abuse, but both of these efforts apply only to cases involving divorce and therefore are not included in this discussion.

Commonalities and Differences Among Guidelines

It is useful to examine commonalities and differences in these 12 schema for decision making. These are presented in Table 11.1. (The authors' names are abbreviated.) Some schema present several criteria, which are subsumed under a single heading in the chart, in which case the number of criteria appears in parentheses after the author's name. For some authors, the opposite of a criterion is deemed characteristic of a true allegation, and this is indicated by a minus sign in parentheses (–) after the name.

There is considerable consistency in what these authors find important to consider. All guidelines include findings from the child interview, and there is general agreement in the field about the centrality of the child interview in sexual abuse evaluations (e.g., Corwin, 1988; De Young, 1986; Faller, 1988, 1990; Faller & Corwin, 1995; Levanthal et al., 1987; Sink, 1988). The most frequently cited factors from the child interview are affect consistent with the abuse description (10) and detail of the sexual abuse (9), and then advanced sexual knowledge (8).

Regarding information from other sources, eight of the guidelines mention medical evidence, seven note nonsexual symptoms, and five note sexualized behavior observed in other settings as important. Only two specify physical evidence that might be gathered from the scene of the crime, for example, an instrument that might have been used or pornography. However, when such evidence is found, it is very important (Faller & Corwin, 1995).

Interestingly, none of the guidelines mention the plethysmograph results or psychological testing of the offender, nor information related to the nonoffending parent or the marriage. However, that may be because these guidelines focus on the probative value of the child interview. Jones and McGraw (1987) are the only authors to refer to the polygraph, and they discount its utility. (See also Saxe, Dougherty, & Cross, [1985]).

Some authors place a great deal of emphasis on factors that seem unimportant to others. For example, Corwin and Sgroi and colleagues emphasize nonsexual symptoms of stress, citing many different ones as indicative of sexual abuse, and CBCA (Raskin & Esplin, 1991; Stellar & Boychuk, 1992; Yuille, 1988) stresses structural aspects of the child's account and contextual factors. In the case of four criteria, authors may hold opposing views. For example, some believe that a reluctance to disclose is characteristic of a true allegation, whereas others look for spontaneity in the child's disclosure as an index of veracity.

Most guidelines do not address the issues of how much information a child must produce or in how many areas confirming information must be found in order to substantiate a case. However, Jones and McGraw (1987) state that the major factor in their determination of sexual abuse is the child's statement that she or he has been sexually abused. Faller (1988) says that behavior or statements about the sexual abuse are both necessary and sufficient for substantiation and discusses both research findings and clinical explanations for why confirming information may be absent in some types of cases. Sink (1988) notes that for a case to be substantiated in the legal arena, Level 1 information must be elicited. However, information from Levels 2 through 4 can be used by a mental health professional to both form an opinion about the likelihood of sexual abuse and plan treatment. The general absence of guidance regarding how much of what kinds of information is necessary to substantiate leaves that decision up to the evaluator.

S T U D Y   Q U E S T I O N S

1. What criteria for assessing an allegation of sexual abuse are most consistent across the 12 guidelines reviewed by the author?
2. What criterion do almost all professionals agree is central to the evaluation?

Berliner and Conte (1993), in a recent review, raise important questions about an "indicators" approach, such as these guidelines use, in making decisions about whether children have been sexually abused. They cite the subjectivity in choices of criteria, discuss certain indicators about which clinicians disagree, and state that the absence of positive indicators does not mean the child has not been sexually abused. They review many of the

TABLE 11.1 Criteria Included in Guidelines for Substantiating Sexual Abuse

	Number	*Author*
Child interview information		
Sexual abuse description	2	B&S, Cor
Detail	9	CBCA, D, F, H, J&M, L, S, SP&B, H, W
Child's perspective	6	B&S (2), F, H (3), J&M, S, W
Advanced sexual knowledge	8	B&S (2), CBCA, Con, Cor (5), F, H, J&M, SP&B
Other	4	B&S (2), Con, J&M, L
Offender behavior description	2	Con, D
Use of inducements to participate	2	B&S, F
Admonitions not to tell	5	B&S, CBCA, D, F, H, L
Progression of abuse	3	B&S, Con, H (2)
Contextual information	4	B&S, CBCA, D, S (2)
Idiosyncratic event	6	CBCA, Con, D, F, H, J&M
Where	3	D, F, L
When	2	D, F
Where others were	1	F, L
Clothing	1	F (2)
Whether told	2	B&S, F (2)
Other	2	CBCA (5), H
Emotional reaction of the child	1	CBCA
Affect consistent with abuse description	10	B&S, CBCA, Con, Cor (2), D, F (6), H (3), J&M, S, W
Affect related to the offender	3	CBCA, Cor, D
Recall of affect during event	5	CBCA, D, F, H, J&M
Reluctance to disclose	6	CBCA (–), Con, Cor (–), F, H, W (–)
Other	3	CBCA, D (3), L
Child functioning		
Competency		
Cognitive testing	2	Con, S
Recall of past	1	B&S, CBCA
Truth from lie	1	B&S
Fact from fantasy	3	B&S, CBCA, Con
Not suggestible	1	H
Motivation to tell the truth	5	B&S, CBCA (2), Con, D, W
Consistency of accounts	7	J&M, Con, CBCA, W (2), D (4, –), H, B&S (–)
Feasibility	3	CBCA, Con, W
Structural qualities of the child's account	4	B&S, CBCA (4), H, W

TABLE 11.1 Continued

	Number	Author
Information from other sources		
Child behavior in other contexts		
Statements to others	5	B&S, F, H, J&M, SP&B
Nonsexual symptoms	7	Con (5), Cor (15), F (6), H (12), J&M, S (3), SP&B (16)
Sexualized behavior	5	Con (4), Cor (3), J&M, SP&B (3), W
Other	2	B&S (2), H (2), S
Offender		
Overall functioning	1	J&M
Results of polygraph	1	J&M (–)
Results of plethysmograph		
Psychological test results		
Other victims	3	F, H, J&M
Confession/admission	1	F
Family		
Information related to nonoffending parent		
Marital functioning		
Family functioning	3	Con (2), H, J&M
Family history of abuse	1	Con
Other		
Medical findings	8	B&S (5), CBCA, Con, F (3), J&M, L, S, W
Police evidence	2	F, H
Witnesses	2	F (2), H

NOTE: B&S = Benedek & Schetky (1987a, 1987b); CBCA = Raskin & Esplin (1991), Stellar & Boychuk (1992), and Yuille (1988); Con = Conte et al. (1991); Cor = Corwin (1988); D = De Young (1986); F = Faller (1984, 1988, 1990, 1993); H = Heiman (1992); J&M = Jones & McGraw (1987); L = Levanthal et al. (1987); S = Sink (1988); SP&B = Sgroi, Porter, and Blick (1982); W = Wehrspann et al. (1987).

guidelines described here and are particularly critical of CBCA and Gardner's Sexual Abuse Legitimacy Scale. They recommend, instead of an indicators approach, addressing the issue of substantiation by reliance on following consensually derived procedures for good practice, for example, as to number of interviews, questioning techniques, and use of media to communicate with the child. Heiman's (1992) work, which specifies domains to be systematically explored, is an effort in this direction.

Despite Berliner and Conte's reservations, both indicators and "procedures" approaches are useful in guiding decisions about child sexual abuse. CBCA is perhaps more limited in its utility than the other strategies because it relies heavily on a spontaneous statement from the child. Research suggests that children are unlikely to provide a spontaneous account of a troubling experience such as sexual abuse (Saywitz et al., 1989). A related point is that CBCA fails to take into account the child's developmental stage and the fact that children of different ages will vary in the amount of detail in their accounts and in the complexity of their linguistic productions.

STUDY QUESTIONS

3. What are some of the main disagreements regarding criteria for assessing an allegation?

   a. What important concerns have been raised about using an indicators approach?

   b. How may the CBCA be especially limited?

References

Benedek, E., & Schetky, D. (1987a). Problems in validating allegations of sexual abuse: Part 1. Factors affecting perception and recall of events. *Journal of the American Academy of Child and Adolescent Psychiatry, 26*, 912-915.

Benedek, E., & Schetky, D. (1987b). Problems in validating allegations of sexual abuse: Part 2. Clinical evaluation. *Journal of the American Academy of Child and Adolescent Psychiatry, 26*, 916-921.

Berliner, L., & Conte, J. (1993). Sexual abuse evaluations: Conceptual and empirical obstacles. *Child Abuse & Neglect, 16*, 111-126.

Conte, J., Sorenson, E., Fogarty, L., & Dalla Rosa, J. (1991). Evaluating children's reports of sexual abuse: Results from a survey of professionals. *American Journal of Orthopsychiatry, 61*, 428-437.

Corwin, D. (1988). Early diagnosis of child sexual abuse: Diminishing the lasting effects. In G. E. Wyatt & G. J. Powell (Eds.), *Lasting effects of child sexual abuse* (pp. 251-270). Newbury Park, CA: Sage.

De Young, M. (1986). A conceptual model for judging the truthfulness of a young child's allegation of sexual abuse. *American Journal of Orthopsychiatry, 56*, 550-559.

Faller, K. C. (1984). Is the child victim of sexual abuse telling the truth? *Child Abuse and Neglect, 8*, 473-481.

Faller, K. C. (1988). Criteria for judging the credibility of children's statements about their sexual abuse. *Child Welfare, 67*, 389-401.

Faller, K. C. (1990). *Understanding child sexual maltreatment.* Newbury Park, CA: Sage.

Faller, K. C. (1993). *Child sexual abuse: Assessment and intervention issues.* Washington, DC: U.S. Department of Health and Human Services, National Center on Child Abuse and Neglect.

Faller, K. C., & Corwin, D. (1995). Children's interview statements and behaviors: Professional consensus and research findings for the identification of sexually abused children. *Child Abuse & Neglect, 19*, 71-82.

Finkelhor, D. (1986). *Sourcebook on child sexual abuse.* Beverly Hills, CA: Sage.

Gardner, R. (1987). *The parental alienation syndrome and the differentiation between fabricated and genuine child sexual abuse.* Cresskill, NJ: Creative Therapeutics.

Gardner, R. (1989). Differentiating between bona fide and fabricated allegations of sexual abuse of children. *Journal of the American Academy of Matrimonial Lawyers, 5*, 1-25.

Green, A. (1986). True and false allegations of sexual abuse in child custody disputes. *Journal of the American Academy of Child and Adolescent Psychiatry, 25*, 449-456.

Heiman, M. (1992). Annotation: Putting the puzzle together: Validating allegations of child sexual abuse. *Journal of Child Psychology and Psychiatry, 33*, 311-329.

Jones, D., & McGraw, E. M. (1987). Reliable and fictitious accounts of sexual abuse to children. *Journal of Interpersonal Violence, 2*, 27-45.

Klajner-Diamond, H., Wehrspann, W., & Steinhauer, P. (1987). Assessing the credibility of young children's allegations of sexual abuse: Clinical issues. *Canadian Journal of Psychiatry, 32*, 610-614.

Levanthal, J., Bentovim, A., Elton, A., Tranter, M., & Read, L. (1987). What to ask when sexual abuse is suspected. *Archives of Disease in Childhood, 62*, 1188-1195.

Raskin, D., & Esplin, P. (1991). Assessment of children's statements of sexual abuse. In J. Doris (Ed.), *The suggestibility of children's recollections.* Washington, DC: American Psychological Association.

Saxe, L., Dougherty, D., & Cross, T. (1985). The validity of polygraph testing: Scientific analysis and public controversy. *American Psychologist, 38*, 355-356.

Saywitz, K., Goodman, G., Nicholas, G., & Moan, S. (1989, April). *Children's memories of genital examinations: Implications for cases of child sexual assault.* Paper presented at the biennial meeting of the Society for Research on Child Development, Kansas City, MO.

Sgroi, S., Porter, F., & Blick, L. (1982). Validation of sexual abuse. In S. Sgroi (Ed.), *Handbook of clinical intervention in child sexual abuse* (pp. 39-80). Lexington, MA: Lexington Books.

Sink, F. (1988). A hierarchical model for evaluation of child sexual abuse. *American Journal of Orthopsychiatry, 58*, 129-135.

Stellar, M., & Boychuk, T. (1992). Children as witnesses in sexual abuse cases: Investigative interview and assessment techniques. In H. Dent & R. Flin (Eds.), *Children as witnesses* (pp. 47-71). Chichester, UK: Wiley.

Undeutch, U. (1989). The development of statement reality analysis. In J. Yuille (Ed.), *Credibility assessment* (pp. 101-119). Dordrecht, Netherlands: Kluwer.

Wehrspann, W., Steinhauer, P., & Klajner-Diamond, H. (1987). Criteria and methodology for assessing credibility of sexual abuse allegation. *Canadian Journal of Psychiatry, 32,* 615-623.

Yuille, J. (1988). The systematic assessment of children's testimony. *Canadian Psychology, 29,* 247-259.

Forming Conclusions

Review and Critique

Mental health professionals evaluating allegations of sexual abuse need to arrive at conclusions, which are then usually memorialized in a written report. These conclusions may also be testified to in court, and the report may be entered into evidence and be the subject of cross-examination. However, some investigative reports, for example, those produced by the Center for Child Protection (1992) and those written by law enforcement, will not offer a conclusion regarding whether the child has been sexually abused.

Because the evaluator's opinion may become part of the court process, the substantive material about which conclusions are formed and exactly how they are stated are important. The court generally will not allow the evaluator to testify as to whether the child is telling the truth because that is the "ultimate legal issue" to be decided by the factfinder (i.e., judge or jury; Melton & Limber, 1989; Myers, 1992). Moreover, the APSAC guidelines (1990) advise the evaluator to communicate that mental health professionals have no special ability to determine when people are telling the truth.

Of course, the reality is that the criteria discussed in the previous section lead to a conclusion about the veracity of an account of sexual abuse, thereby leading indirectly to a conclusion about the truthfulness of the child. Moreover, if the evaluator concludes the child's account is probably true, the child has named an offender, and the offender denies, then the evaluator has indirectly formed a conclusion about the truthfulness of the alleged offender's assertions. Nevertheless, the evaluator is advised to be cautious about including in his or her written report an opinion regarding the truthfulness of either the child or the alleged offender.

On the other hand, the evaluator can draw a conclusion about whether the child has been sexually abused (AACAP, 1990; APSAC, 1990). At this point, the majority opinion is that the evaluator can do so (Myers, 1992); however, Melton and Limber (1989) disagree. The APSAC guidelines provide alternative ways of expressing this conclusion. They advise that the evaluator may state either that she or he believes the abuse did or did not occur, that the child's statement or behavior is consistent or inconsistent with abuse, or with a history or the absence of a history of sexual abuse. However, as already noted, the Center for Child Protection (1992) protocol instructs the evaluator to merely cite information obtained during the assessment that is supportive or not supportive of sexual abuse, but not state directly whether the evaluator believes the child has been sexually abused.

STUDY QUESTIONS

1. Why should a conclusion regarding the truthfulness of the child or alleged offender be approached with caution?
   a. Where does the court stand on this issue?
   b. How does APSAC suggest the evaluator express her or his opinion?

An important question to address is the degree of certainty the evaluator has about the conclusions. Jones and McGraw (1987) have developed a useful framework—a continuum of certainty—for addressing this issue. In very few cases will the evaluator be absolutely sure sexual abuse did or did not occur, and it is probably inadvisable to make an absolute statement in most cases. The language employed by the evaluator should reflect the degree of certainty the evaluator has about the likelihood of sexual abuse in the case under consideration (Faller, 1993). Moreover, given the research demonstrating the substantial proportion of false negatives (Faller, 1988; Lawson & Chaffin, 1992; Saywitz et al., 1989; Sorenson & Snow, 1991) and the cautionary comments of Conte and colleagues (1991) regarding indicators of sexual abuse, evaluators are advised to consider the use of language such as "sexual abuse could not be substantiated," rather than "sexual abuse did not occur."

It is important for evaluators to state not only their conclusions but also the evidence employed in reaching them (AACAP, 1990; APSAC, 1990; Faller, 1993). This should include information from all sources, not merely the child interview(s). Child interview data should include verbatim statements and behavioral observations. This is one reason why it is important to have good documentation of the interview (e.g., a video- or audiotape). It is useful to chronicle the information gathered and then separately state the conclusions or opinion, referring back to supporting evidence.

S T U D Y   Q U E S T I O N S

2. What is meant by a continuum of certainty?

   How should the evaluator's language reflect this continuum?

3. What types of evidence should the evaluator cite in the formation of her or his opinion?

   How should this evidence be incorporated into the report?

Sometimes, the evaluation is inconclusive. Both the APSAC and AACAP guidelines point out that the evaluator may not be able to form a conclusion and should so state and document the reasons why.

A number of professionals (Faller, 1993; James, Everson, & Friedrich, n.d.) recommend an extended evaluation in such circumstances. Some see this as a strategy to be used with young children who lack communication skills (James et al., n.d.). It consists of 6 to 18 months of therapy, during which the child matures in language and communication ability, and after which a forensic interview is conducted. Others (Faller, 1993) use extended evaluations for children who are reluctant to disclose. In this instance, the extended evaluation consists of as many as six interviews during which the possibility of sexual abuse is raised with the child in a variety of ways.

Sometimes, environmental manipulations, such as foster care placement or stopping visits with the alleged offender, are used to increase the child's comfort and enhance the likelihood of disclosure.

Professionals face significant dilemmas regarding protection of children when the evaluation is inconclusive. The need to foster attachment between parent and child may be in conflict with the issue of safety. In this regard, Hewitt (1991) has proposed a sensible case management strategy, which she implemented in seven inconclusive cases of allegations of sexual abuse in divorce with young children. Briefly, she conducted interviews with the child, each parent, and each parent-child dyad. In the dyadic sessions, she had each parent communicate to the child what parts of the body should not be touched and had the accused parent give the child permission to tell if he engaged in sexually inappropriate behavior with the child. The nonaccused parent was instructed, when indicated, in how to listen to the child and ask questions in a nonleading manner. Initially, visits with the child and accused parent were supervised and then the child was monitored for at least 1 year with unsupervised visits. In a 5-year follow-up, there were no complaints of subsequent abuse in six cases, and questionable, but not clearly abusive, behavior in one. Although Hewitt's strategy does not speak to all cases where children are at risk, such innovative practice is precisely what the child sexual abuse field needs.

STUDY QUESTIONS

4. How does the evaluator report to the court when she or he is unable to form a conclusion?

   a. When the evaluation is inconclusive, what other options may the evaluator consider?

   b. How can the issue of child protection be addressed in such cases?

References

American Academy of Child and Adolescent Psychiatry (AACAP). (1990, December). *Guidelines for the evaluation of child and adolescent sexual abuse.* (Available from AACAP, 3615 Wisconsin Ave. N.W., Washington, DC 20016)

American Professional Society on the Abuse of Children (APSAC). (1990). *Guidelines for psychosocial evaluation of suspected sexual abuse in young children.* (Available from APSAC, 332 S. Michigan Ave., Chicago, IL 60604)

Center for Child Protection. (1992). *Sexual abuse evidentiary protocol.* (Available from the Center for Child Protection, Children's Hospital and Health Center, San Diego, CA 92123)

Conte, J., Sorenson, E., Fogarty, L., & Dalla Rosa, J. (1991). Evaluating children's reports of sexual abuse: Results from a survey of professionals. *American Journal of Orthopsychiatry, 61,* 428-437.

Faller, K. C. (1988). Criteria for judging the credibility of children's statements about their sexual abuse. *Child Welfare, 67,* 389-401.

Faller, K. C. (1993). *Child sexual abuse: Assessment and intervention issues.* Washington, DC: U.S. Department of Health and Human Services, National Center on Child Abuse and Neglect.

Hewitt, S. (1991). Therapeutic management of preschool cases of alleged but unsubstantiated sexual abuse. *Child Welfare, 70,* 59-67.

James, B., Everson, M., & Friedrich, W. (n.d.). *Extended evaluations of allegations of child sexual abuse.* (Available from Beverly James, James Institute, P.O. Box 148, Honolulu, HI 96726)

Jones, D., & McGraw, E. M. (1987). Reliable and fictitious accounts of sexual abuse to children. *Journal of Interpersonal Violence, 2,* 27-45.

Lawson, L., & Chaffin, M. (1992). False negatives in sexual abuse disclosure interviews. *Journal of Interpersonal Violence, 7,* 532-542.

Melton, G., & Limber, S. (1989). Psychologists' involvement in cases of child maltreatment. *American Psychologist, 44,* 1225-1233.

Myers, J. E. B. (1992). *Legal issues in child abuse and neglect.* Newbury Park, CA: Sage.

Saywitz, K., Goodman, G., Nicholas, G., & Moan, S. (1989. April). *Children's memories of genital examinations: Implications for cases of child sexual assault.* Paper presented at the biennial meeting of the Society for Research on Child Development, Kansas City, MO.

Sorenson, T., & Snow, B. (1991). How children tell: The process of disclosure in child sexual abuse. *Child Welfare, 70*(1), 3-15.

About the Author

Kathleen Coulborn Faller, PhD, ACSW, is Professor of Social Work at the University of Michigan. She is also Director of the Family Assessment Clinic, a multidisciplinary team that evaluates cases of child maltreatment, codirector of the Interdisciplinary Project on Child Abuse and Neglect, and faculty coordinator of the Civitas Partnership, all at the University of Michigan.

She is involved in research, clinical work, teaching, training, and writing in the area of child sexual abuse. She is the author of *Social Work With Abused and Neglected Children* (1981), *Child Sexual Abuse: An Interdisciplinary Manual for Diagnosis, Case Management, and Treatment* (Columbia University Press, 1988), *Understanding Child Sexual Maltreatment* (Sage, 1990), and *Child Sexual Abuse: Assessment and Intervention Issues* (U.S. Department of Health and Human Services, National Center on Child Abuse and Neglect, 1993), as well as a number of research studies and clinical articles in the area of child sexual abuse.

She is presently a member of the board of directors and of the executive committee of the American Professional Society on the Abuse of Children (APSAC).

Evaluating Children Suspected of Having Been Sexually Abused

Checklist for Continuing Education Credits

To be eligible to receive 7 CE credits for this program, the following must be completed and returned to the following address:

PsychoEducational Resources
P.O. Box 2196
Keystone Heights, FL 32656

—— A completed knowledge test

—— A completed "Client Vignette" form

—— A signed statement (below) verifying your completion of this home study program

—— A completed program evaluation/participant satisfaction form (see below)

Your name as you want it to appear on your CE certificate: _____

Address: _____ Degree:_____

_____ Discipline: _____

_____ Date: _____

I confirm that I personally have completed the above test, and I am submitting it for CE certification.

Signature: _____

Evaluation of Program

Please circle the appropriate response to each of the items below. Your feedback will be used by PER to evaluate the appropriateness of this form of home study as a Continuing Education activity and will provide guidance in the selection and development of future offerings in the video series.

	Strongly Agree		Neutral		Strongly Disagree
The content of the program was informative for a professional at my level of training.	1	2	3	4	5
The material included in this program was appropriate to my learning objectives.	1	2	3	4	5
The questions comprising the CE quiz fairly tested my knowledge of the program materials.	1	2	3	4	5
I would be interested in participating in similar CE offerings in the future.	1	2	3	4	5

Estimate of amount of time required for study of all materials and completion of CE tests: _____

Suggestions for future topics:

Evaluating Children Suspected of Having Been Sexually Abused

KNOWLEDGE TEST

To be eligible to receive 7 Continuing Education credits for this home study module, please complete the knowledge test below, circling the letter of the correct response to each item. You must respond correctly to at least 80% of the items to pass.

1. The behavioral checklist most widely used with both sexually abused and otherwise maltreated children is the _____.
   a. Louisville Behavior Checklist
   b. Achenbach Child Behavior Checklist
   c. Trauma Symptom Checklist for Children
   d. Sexual Abuse Symptom Checklist

2. With regard to sexual abuse victim characteristics, Everson, Boat, and Robertson (1992) found that _____ children were judged more believable than _____ ones.
   a. passive; aggressive
   b. aggressive; passive
   c. younger; older
   d. older; younger

3. The findings regarding the effect of stress on memory are _____.
   a. clear, with researchers finding that stress decreases the accuracy of recall
   b. clear, with researchers finding that stress increases the accuracy of recall
   c. clear, with researchers finding that stress does not affect the accuracy of recall
   d. mixed, with some researchers finding that stress decreases the accuracy of recall and others not

4. Reports indicate that most false accusations are made by _____ children who appeared to make the allegations for _____ gain.
   a. younger; primary
   b. younger; secondary
   c. older; primary
   d. older; secondary

5. In comparing the relative impact of anatomical drawings, verbal descriptions, anatomical dolls, and a computer-assisted interview on children's ability to recount medical procedures, Steward (1989) found anatomical drawings to be superior to _____, but not superior to _____.
   a. verbal questioning; other media
   b. anatomical dolls; computer-assisted interview
   c. computer-assisted interview; verbal questioning
   d. anatomical dolls; verbal questioning

115

6. In a study by Hibbard, Roghmann, and Hoekelman (1987), it was found that 3- to 7-year-old children assessed for sexual abuse were _____ times more likely to draw genitalia than their nonabused counterparts.
   a. one to two
   b. two to four
   c. four to six
   d. six to eight

7. According to Hewitt (1993), children's memory _____ the time when they can verbally communicate it.
   a. precedes
   b. immediately follows
   c. distantly follows
   d. coincides with

8. According to Faller, the only way of knowing definitely that sexual abuse did not happen is _____.
   a. the child recants the allegation
   b. the nonaccused custodial parent cannot substantiate the allegation
   c. there was no opportunity for the accused to have access to the child
   d. the accused does not match any criteria established as the typical offender profile

9. Although Friedrich (1994) has observed that sexualized behavior is the most frequently found marker of sexual abuse, it is present in only about _____ of children believed to have been sexually abused.
   a. 10%
   b. 20%
   c. 30%
   d. 40%

10. Recently, Merry, Franzep, and Andrews (1994) investigated the psychiatric status of children 12 months after the disclosure of sexual abuse and found that _____ were assessed with psychiatric diagnoses on the *DSM-III-R*.
    a. 29.5%
    b. 49.5%
    c. 69.5%
    d. 89.5%

11. The majority of sexual abuse investigations include _____ child interview(s).
    a. one
    b. three
    c. five
    d. seven

12. According to Faller, an important factor to assess in determining the relevance of research on child reports of sexual abuse is its _____ validity.
    a. internal
    b. ecological
    c. construct
    d. concurrent

13. Recently, Hewitt and Arrowood (1994) described a potentially useful drawing task called the Touch Continuum. Findings, based on a comparison of this technique to a comprehensive assessment of possible sexual abuse, showed no _____ positives from the Touch Continuum data, but a high rate of _____ negatives.
    a. true; true
    b. true; false
    c. false; true
    d. false; false

14. According to Faller, most researchers have used one of the following strategies for identifying false allegations *except* _____.
    a. recantation by the child
    b. consensually arrived at criteria
    c. a disposition by a mandated professional
    d. the author's clinical judgment

15. Sgroi, Porter, and Blick (1982) were among the first professionals to offer guidance about deciding if children have been sexually abused, focusing on such behavioral indicators as all of the following *except* _____.
    a. overly compliant behavior
    b. overly passive behavior
    c. pseudomature behavior
    d. inappropriate sexual play with peers, toys, or themselves

16. According to Sorenson and Snow (1991), older children are more likely to _____ disclose and younger children to _____ disclose.
    a. maliciously; malevolently
    b. malevolently; maliciously
    c. accidentally; intentionally
    d. intentionally; accidentally

17. The limited research that compares the proportion of false allegations generated by adults and children indicates that adults are _____ to make such allegations.
    a. more likely
    b. less likely
    c. equally likely
    d. very unlikely

18. Conte, Sorenson, Fogarty, and Dalla Rosa (1991) found that _____ of experts in their study employ psychological tests during the course of evaluations.
    a. 14%
    b. 28%
    c. 42%
    d. 56%

19. In most studies cited by Faller, children have been found to be more likely to make errors of _____ than errors of _____.
    a. commission; omission
    b. omission; commission
    c. time; place
    d. place; time

20. In a recent study by Oates, O'Toole, Lynch, Stern, and Cooney (1994), it was found that the major variable relating to improvement in sexually abused children appears to be _____.
    a. adequacy of family functioning
    b. the relationship between the child and the abuser
    d. psychotherapy for the child
    e. psychotherapy for the abuser

21. According to research cited in this study guide, children older than _____ years old have memories as good as those of adults.
    a. 3
    b. 5
    c. 8
    d. 10

22. When assessing for possible sexual abuse, Faller (1991, 1993) proposes a continuum of questions in the following order: _____ questions.
    a. leading, general, multiple choice, yes-no, focused
    b. general, leading, yes-no, multiple choice, focused
    c. general, focused, multiple choice, yes-no, leading
    d. focused, general, multiple choice, yes-no, leading

23. According to the American Association for Protecting Children (1988), as well as McCurdy and Daro (1994), nationally, between _____ of reported sexual abuse cases are not substantiated.
    a. 10% to 25%
    b. 30% to 45%
    c. 50% to 65%
    d. 70% to 85%

24. A goal in the management of sexual abuse cases is to _____ different professionals who interview the child.
    a. minimize the number of
    b. maximize the number of
    c. have two to four
    d. have more than five

25. When considering the relative advantages and disadvantages of anatomical drawings and anatomical dolls, the drawings may be of _____ utility than the dolls as a diagnostic screen or a memory stimulus, and of _____ use as part of the case record.
    a. greater; greater
    b. greater; lesser
    c. lesser; greater
    d. lesser; lesser

26. Of the advantages of videotaping interviews, as elaborated by Myers (1992), which of the following was *not* cited? _____.
    a. It may decrease the number of interviews
    b. It could be used to persuade the offender to confess
    c. It may decrease the probability of recantation
    d. It could allow further questioning on inconsistencies

27. Brainerd and Ornstein (1991) have found that young children have better recall of _____ events in their lives than of _____ ones.
    a. peripheral; salient
    b. salient; peripheral
    c. repeated; salient
    d. peripheral; repeated

28. The APSAC guidelines regarding the documentation indicate that at minimum there should be _____, and the use of _____ should be determined by professional preference, logistics, and clinical considerations.
    a. audiotapes; videotapes
    b. videotapes; audiotapes
    c. written notes; audio- or videotapes
    d. audio- or videotapes; written notes

29. In contrast to the difficulty of determining unequivocally that an allegation is false, evaluators can be virtually certain that sexual abuse did, in fact, occur when any of the following are present *except* _____.
    a. a confession by the accused
    b. a reliable eyewitness
    c. a prior conviction of the accused for sexual abuse
    d. pornography involving the victim

30. New studies comparing sexually abused girls to controls have revealed all of the following differences *except* the following: _____.
    a. Controls mature earlier than sexually abused girls
    b. The two groups had different hormonal responses
    c. Sexually abused girls may develop impaired immune functioning
    d. Sexually abused girls had higher levels of urinary catecholamine

31. After examining the accounts of sexual abuse of 18 children victimized by a single offender who confessed, Terry (1991) found that on average the children recounted about _____ of the activities mentioned by the offender.
    a. 20%
    b. 40%
    c. 60%
    d. 80%

32. Using free drawings, Yates, Beutler, and Crago (1985) found that sexually abused girls were likely to either _____ the sexual parts of the body or to _____ them.
    a. maximize; enlarge
    b. exaggerate; maximize
    c. minimize; avoid
    d. exaggerate; avoid

33. According to the research of Conte and colleagues (1991), _____ are the most widely used medium in interviewing children suspected of being sexually abused.
    a. anatomical dolls
    b. anatomical drawings
    c. picture drawings by the child
    d. picture drawings by the interviewer

34. When considering criteria included in the guidelines offered by a variety of authors for substantiating sexual abuse, although both commonalities and differences emerge, all guidelines include findings from _____.
    a. the observation of sexual acting out
    b. the physical evidence gathered from the scene of the alleged crime
    c. the child interview
    d. the results of psychological testing of the accused

35. After their review of previous studies of children's sexualized behavior with anatomical dolls, as well as their own research, Everson and Boat (1990) concluded that anatomical dolls _____ appear to provide sexually naive children a stimulus to engage in sexualized doll play and that they _____ appear to provide sexually knowledgeable children the same opportunity.
    a. do; do
    b. do; do not
    c. do not; do
    d. do not; do not

36. In general, studies investigating the effectiveness of the use of anatomical dolls have found that these dolls _____ children's responses to abuse-related queries when compared to questioning without props and that they _____ superior to nonanatomical dolls or other media.
    a. improve; are
    b. improve; are not
    c. reduce; are
    d. reduce; are not

37. Everson and Boat (1994) have found that although views among professionals differ regarding how to use anatomical dolls, there is fairly wide support for their use as an anatomical model and a _____.
    a. subjective psychological test
    b. projective test
    c. demonstration aid
    d. memory enhancer

38. Of the following specific drawing tasks that might elicit information relevant to sexual abuse, which is likely to yield the *least* clear data to substantiate a claim of abuse? _____.
    a. drawings of the alleged offender
    b. drawings of the victim herself or himself
    c. drawings of an instrument that might have been used in the abuse
    d. drawings of the place where the abuse is thought to have occurred

39. The guidelines for the evaluation of suspected sexual abuse published by APSAC are applicable for cases of _____ sexual abuse, whereas those published by AACAP seem intended for _____ sexual abuse cases.
    a. extrafamilial; both intrafamilial and extrafamilial
    b. intrafamilial; both intrafamilial and extrafamilial
    c. both intrafamilial and extrafamilial; extrafamilial
    d. both intrafamilial and extrafamilial; intrafamilial

40. In a study investigating the factors related to trauma in childhood sexual abuse, Mennen and Meadow (1994) have found that sexually abused girls had _____ than their nonabused counterparts.
    a. lower levels of anxiety
    b. lower levels of depression
    c. lower levels of self-worth
    d. all of the above

To gain greater familiarity with the practical implications of this study guide, try applying what you have learned to the following hypothetical counseling scenario. The questions that follow should help you think through your interventions with a child whose mother wants her assessed for possible sexual abuse and incorporate the material in this guide into your work as a counselor or therapist.

CLIENT VIGNETTE

Susie M. is a 6-year-old girl whose mother contacted you regarding her unusual behavior. Over the past few months, Susie has become exceedingly fearful of men, as evidenced by her running away from all males who try to approach her. Susie's mother has also noticed that Susie has not been sleeping as well as she had in the past, showing difficulties falling asleep as well as multiple awakenings during the night. Additionally, Susie's first-grade teacher has reportedly contacted her mother the previous week, stating that Susie has been caught several times over the past few weeks displaying her genitals to her classmates. Susie's mother, who is legally separated and lives apart from Susie's father, has become concerned that she has been sexually abused. (Attach additional pages as needed for responses to Client Vignette questions.)

CLIENT VIGNETTE 1

1. What types of questions would you ask Susie and her mother regarding Susie's symptomatology to evaluate the possibility of sexual abuse? What other factors might be relevant to your diagnostic impression? What information might convince you that the possibility of abuse should be disconfirmed?

CLIENT VIGNETTE 1, *continued*

2. Assume that you have come to the conclusion that Susie has, in fact, been sexually abused. What kind of treatment plan might you develop to support her recovery? To what extent would you involve her mother in this treatment plan?

CLIENT VIGNETTE 2, *continued*

CLIENT VIGNETTE 3

3. Suppose that Susie refuses to talk to you about the incident. What medium(s) would you employ to elicit noncoerced responses?

CLIENT VIGNETTE 3, *continued*